Guiding Light

Feed My Soul
CYCLE C

Homilies by Fr. Joe Robinson

Shepherds of Christ Publications
P.O. Box 627
China, Indiana 47250 USA

Toll free USA: (888) 211-3041
Tel: (812) 273-8405
Fax: (812) 273-3182
Email: info@sofc.org
http://www.sofc.org

ISBN: 978-1-934222-27-0

First Printing: 2009

In honor

of our

Beloved Priests

Table of Contents
Cycle C

Foreward

For years all of us have gone to St. Boniface Church in Cincinnati, Ohio. Our family first lived in this parish – Some of the streets named after our relatives –

Fr. Carter was the founder of the Shepherds of Christ Movement and I, Rita Ring, co-founder –

But my brother, Fr. Joseph Robinson was an important part of my life and our lives as we went to his most holy Masses and listened to his homilies as we formed more and more as a body of people producing the Priestly Newsletter and beginning prayer chapters.

God blessed me and all of us being able to go to his Masses and listen to his homilies –

It is a tremendous honor Fr. Joe has allowed us to share these great gifts with you – for greater holiness and knowing more and more about God –

This is the first of a series of these books – dedicated to our priests, out of love for our beloved Church and all the souls of the world.

As you use these great teachings of homilies Sunday after Sunday – please pray the prayers with us as a network of prayer – praying for the priests, the Church and the world –

I thank God every day for the gift of my older brother who has been an important instrument in his priesthood in my life and the lives of all who went to St. Boniface for Mass.

Rita Ring
Co-founder, Shepherds of Christ Movement

1st Sunday of Advent
December 3, 2006

INTRODUCTION – (Jer 33:14-16; 1 Thess 3:12 – 4:2; Luke 21:25-28, 34-36) The prophet, Jeremiah, lived during one of the most devastating times in the history of Israel. He witnessed the destruction of Jerusalem and the Temple by the Babylonians. He saw many of his fellow citizens enslaved and taken into exile. Yet his words reflect hope and not despair. His hope is based not on human capabilities but on God's faithfulness to God's promises. Jeremiah recalls God's promise to his people made over 400 years earlier, during the time of King David, that God would bring to the throne a successor to the King who would bring peace and security to Jerusalem. We still wait for peace and security not only in Jerusalem but all over the world, but the promised one, a descendant of the House of David has begun his reign. The gospel tells us one day he will come in great glory to establish the kingdom of God forever.

HOMILY – Although our society has begun its preparations for the birth of Christ, even as they are hesitant to mention his birth, the Church begins its preparations today. Our liturgy, however, wants us to know that we are not only preparing for a special celebration three weeks from now, but our readings put before us the bigger picture. It's not just the celebration of Jesus' birth that we are to prepare for but also we must prepare for the day when he comes again to bring us into his kingdom. Advent tells us Christ is coming, but it also asks us, are we ready to meet him? If we're not, his coming 2000 years ago will have little or no value for us.

For some people his second coming will be a frightening time. "People will die in fright in anticipation of what is coming upon the world..." But if we are prepared, not just for Christmas, but for Christ, the Lord tells us "stand erect and raise your heads because your redemption is at hand." His coming will be for those who have followed him faithfully a day of victory and joy.

Doesn't it sound as if our Lord is speaking to us today when he tells us: "Be on guard lest your spirits become bloated with indulgence and drunkenness and worldly cares." We have to struggle against this happening to all of us during this time of the year. I'm going to add a thought of my own to this list of things Jesus tells us to guard against. Make sure to get enough rest. When we are tired it's hard to stay organized, focused, to keep our priorities straight and to pray. And if we don't pray and keep our priorities straight, Christmas will leave us feeling empty and relieved that it's all over.

The gospel's suggestion for us today as we begin Advent is: "Be vigilant at all times and pray..." Is there a better formula we can apply to this season to prepare for the celebration of Christ's birth or the coming of Christ at the end of our lives or at the end of time. I'm not going around like Scrooge saying "Bah, humbug!" to Christmas. I like decorations and lights and parties and Christmas cards and gifts, but to prepare ourselves for what this season of the year is all about, nothing will do the job better than prayer and good works.

You might pray the rosary or meditate on the Scripture readings for each day. They are printed every week in the bulletin and you will find them also in the Catholic Update inserted in today's bulletin. We have Mass here every morning at 7:30 and Holy Hour twice a week. We have a bible study, a Legion of Mary, a St. Vincent de Paul, the CAIN ministry and, of course, Bingo. There's no end of other good works anyone can find to do if they are interested. This year we have the shortest Advent possible (only three weeks), so I hope we all make the most of it.

And now is the time to do it. No doubt you've heard this poem before, but it won't hurt to repeat it. It is entitled Today:

I shall do much in the years to come, but what have I done today?

I shall give out gold in princely sum, but what did I give today?

I shall lift the heart and dry the tear,

I shall plant a hope in the place of fear,

I shall speak with words of love and cheer, but what have I done today?

I shall be so kind in the after while, but what have I been today?

I shall bring to each lonely life a smile, but what have I brought today?

I shall give to truth a grander birth,

And to steadfast faith a deeper worth,

I shall feed the hungering souls of earth, but whom have I fed today?

Feast of the Immaculate Conception
December 8, 2005

HOMILY – (Gen. 3, 9–15, 20; Luke 1, 26–38) The feast today is about Mary's conception, that from the instant she began to exist on this earth, indeed from her very conception, she was holy, filled with God's grace and without sin. The gospel today can confuse us somewhat because it tells us about Jesus' conception. It was read today, first of all, because there is no gospel telling us about the moment when Mary was conceived. And secondly today's gospel does give us an important piece of information about Mary related to today's feast. The angel greeted her as: "Full of grace." Our feast celebrates what the angel stated. There was no moment in Mary's life when God's grace did not fill her. She was full of grace.

As we listen in on this conversation between Mary and the Angel, we learn not only about Mary but also about the child she is going to have. Mary's son to be would be Son of the Most High and king forever. Her child will be called "holy, the Son of God." In the midst of all our business, we pause on this Holy Day to think what it is we are happy about at this time of year.

This is why Mary was "full of grace," so she could give birth to the source of all holiness and grace, God's own Son. And why did he come to us? So that we too can become holy. This is what St. Paul tells us in today's second reading: "God chose us in him to be holy and blameless in his sight."

Holiness is something few people strive for. All of us want to get to heaven, but most of us would probably tend to say I just want to get inside the door. We should do more than just try to get inside the door. We are called to be holy. Most of us never think that becoming holy is our vocation. We usually think holiness is for someone else, like the saints or people in religious orders. That's because we do not understand holiness. We think being holy means spending all day praying or wearing ourselves out doing good things for others and never having a chance to have any fun. I think holy people probably have as much fun as any of us, but there's something greater than fun. It is joy and peace and love. To be holy means to be close to God. The closer we are to God, the more we will be filled with love and joy and peace – both in this life and throughout eternity.

Our vocation to holiness is illustrated by the two stories we heard today.

The first story was about our first parents who originally were very close to God and were very happy. That was the symbolism of the Garden of Eden. But that wasn't good enough for them. They wanted to be like God himself. So they rebelled against God and they lost all they had.

The second story, the annunciation, illustrates Mary's constant attitude of being willing to say "yes" to God. It was only through her openness that the Son of the Most High has come to us. St. Luke tells us Mary was not only holy and always ready to do whatever God wanted of her, but he also tells us she was joyful. Holiness and joy are connected. After the angel left Mary, St. Luke told us about Mary visiting her cousin and she was full of joy. She expressed her joy in the beautiful hymn "the Magnificat." My soul gives glory to the Lord and my spirit rejoices in God my savior."

In reflecting on the holiness of Mary, we may feel as if we were treated unfairly. We were born with original sin. The deck was stacked against us from the beginning. But we forget that when we were baptized we were filled with God's life. The very same grace that filled Mary at the moment of her conception, filled us when we were baptized. So holiness is possible for us too. Our two stories can show us there are two ways each of us can go in life. We can follow the example of our first parents, Adam and Eve, or we can follow the example of Mary. The first will lead to sorrow, the other to joy. To imitate Mary, all we have to do is say "yes" to whatever God asks of us.

2nd Sunday of Advent
December 10, 2006

INTRODUCTION – (Bar 5:1-9; Phil 1:4-6, 8-11; Luke 3:1-6) In today's first reading, we hear from Baruch, the secretary of Jeremiah the prophet and apparently a prophet himself. He lived during the Babylonian exile over 500 years before Christ. When the Babylonians conquered Jerusalem, they destroyed everything and took most of its citizens to Babylon as captives. The prophet Baruch addresses Jerusalem and tells the city to rejoice, God will bring back the captives and Jerusalem will prosper again.

HOMILY – Father Joseph Donders who lives in Washington DC tells an interesting story about going to the airport to pick up a friend who was coming to visit him from Africa. It was a cold, winter day and all the trees were bare except for a few firs and the pines. This was the first time his friend had ever left his home country in Africa. As he looked at the trees he said, "I had heard about this, but I did not realize things were so bad." Not knowing what his African friend was talking about, Fr. Donders asked "What do you mean?" His friend said he heard about air pollution in America and its effect on the trees, "but," he said, "I never thought it was bad as this with all those trees dead!"

In the part of Africa where his visitor came from, the trees were always green and most of the time in full bloom. Some trees would lose their leaves for brief periods throughout the year but never all at once as happens here in the fall and winter in the United States. So the visitor from Africa presumed air pollution had killed them all.

Two men saw the same thing and yet their view was entirely different. One saw only death and destruction, the other saw nothing of the kind, for he could see beyond the winter to springtime and new life. Our readings today demonstrate a similar event. Baruch, in today's first reading, is speaking to God's people during the upheaval of the Babylonian exile. He tells them God is ready to bring the exiles back home, and the return home will be a glorious event. By this time the people had lost hope that Jerusalem would ever be rebuilt, and the exiles believed they would be spending the rest of their lives as captives in a foreign land. The prophet saw beyond their present captivity to a glorious future.

The Jews at the time of John the Baptist, 500 years later, were not a free people. They had their Temple; Jerusalem had been rebuilt. But they were part of the great Roman Empire. Rome made the rules, Rome collected their taxes (and they were heavily taxed), Roman soldiers marched through their streets and a Roman governor who was noted for his brutality, named Pontius Pilate, controlled their land. Most of us think of Pilate as sympathetic or just plain weak because of the way he handled Jesus when Jesus was arrested. Most of us do not know that in a couple of years Pilate would lose his job because his Roman bosses, who were not nice people themselves, considered him too ruthless and violent. But the prophet John the Baptist saw beyond all their oppression as he quotes from the prophet Isaiah: "all flesh shall see the salvation of God."

In our own day there are enough things going on to depress us if we dwell on them all. It might be world events, it might be the social and moral climate we live in, it might be personal agonies or worries. Sometimes we need help to see beyond our present woes, someone who can give us hope, someone who is a prophet who can tells us spring will soon be here and the trees will be in full bloom again.

This is what our readings are telling us. This is what Jesus' birth is telling us. This is what his presence with us today in the Eucharist is telling us. But today's readings are telling us one more thing. They are telling us we can't just sit back and wait for it all to happen. We have to prepare. Quoting Isaiah, the Baptist cries out to prepare the way of the Lord.

There is a danger that when I say the word "prepare" most people will start thinking "yeah! I have tons of things to get ready!" Suddenly I'll lose their attention while they're making their list and checking it twice thinking of all the things they have to do. That's not what it's all about. The springtime that we have to look forward to depends on our willingness to open our lives to it through faith or we will remain in the cold and dark. The new life we hope for comes to us only when we submit our lives to Jesus as our Lord and Savior.

So when I say prepare, I want you to look into your lives more deeply than thinking of decorations or parties or gifts or cards. Those are nice, but there's more to it. St. Paul today gives us an idea of what we should be doing to prepare when he tells the Philippians what he prays for them. He prays that their love for God and for each other may increase, that they keep a sense of what is important in life and that they live pure and blameless lives filled with good works. That is my prayer for you too. Amen.

3rd Sunday of Advent
December 17, 2006

INTRODUCTION – (Zeph 3:14-18a; Phil 4:4-7; Luke 3:10-18) Our theme for today, as it often is, is summed up in the Psalm Refrain: "Cry out with joy and gladness, for among you is the great and holy one of Israel." Our first reading from the prophet Zephaniah goes back about 700 years before Christ. The Assyrians were the dominant force in the Middle East and were an unusually warlike, brutal people. Their capital city was in northern Iraq near modern day Mosul. Our first reading comes from a time shortly after the Assyrians wiped out the northern part of Israel. They brought severe suffering upon the southern part of Israel too, the area around Jerusalem, but they did not conquer it. Jerusalem would still stand for another 130 years until the Babylonians conquered it. The Babylonian empire, as you might remember, was centered around Baghdad and it was after they destroyed the Assyrian empire that they moved on to conquer many other nations in the Middle East which included Judah and Jerusalem. (It sounds very much like what's going on over there today, doesn't it?) Meanwhile back to Zephaniah 700 years before Christ after the northern part of Israel had been devastated. Jerusalem was struggling to recover from the near destruction they had suffered, but they didn't learn their lesson. Idolatry and immorality were rampant among the Jews. The king of Judah himself offered his own son as a human sacrifice to the pagan gods. Most of Zephaniah's book records his efforts to correct abuses among God's people. His book ends on a note of hope, however, as he addresses those who are faithful to God. He tells them to rejoice and assures them God will rejoice and sing too because of his love for them and for all the blessings that will be theirs. Can any of us begin to imagine what it would sound like to hear God singing?

There is something we should be aware of when we hear the second reading too. St. Paul is sitting in prison somewhere when he wrote this, and prisons in those days were really bad. Today's prisons would look like a luxury hotel by comparison. Yet Paul can be joyful and he is able to encourage the Philippians to have no anxiety and to rejoice always.

HOMILY – In the days when we had Mass in Latin, today was known as Gaudete Sunday. That means "Be Joyful." The liturgy continues to communicate that theme of joy with rose colored vestments and readings telling us to rejoice.

So on this Gaudete Sunday I thought you would enjoy a couple of laughs.

First a riddle for you: Why is Christmas just like a day at the office? Answer: You do all the work, and the guy that wears that big fancy suit gets all the credit.

A couple were always fascinated by old churches and wherever they traveled if they came near an old church they had to stop and look inside. Once in a small town church they saw an oddly shaped bell and asked the person cleaning the church what the strange bell was used for. They were told "That bell is reserved for calamities, like fires, floods, or a visit from the archbishop."

Lastly, if laughter really were the best medicine, hospitals would have found a way to charge us for it long ago.

Laughter fades away, but there is something that lasts and sustains us all the more: joy. Joy goes deeper than just being funny. We heard the prophet in today's first reading telling God's people, during an especially difficult time in their history, to "sing for joy." They should sing for joy not because things were wonderful, but because God was in their midst. And we heard Paul, in prison, tell the Philippians to rejoice always. The scriptures give us different ideas about joy than our culture does. Our society seems to tell us joy stems from what we have. The scriptures tell us our joy comes from what we have (for the Lord is in your midst as Zephaniah tells us) but it also comes from what we will have in some future time, something we can trust in because God is faithful to his promises.

In the few minutes I have, let me name some of the things that keep us from having joy: * Feeling sorry for oneself. * Constantly putting other people down to make ourselves look smarter or better. * Putting ourselves down all the time. Because we're human we all make mistakes or do wrong and there are healthy ways of dealing with guilty or shame, but constantly beating ourselves up is not one of them. * Holding on to anger and resentment. It only eats us up inside and does not produce joy. We have to forgive. * Thinking that having more things is going to make us happy. It satisfies us only momentarily. * And then there's fear and worry. Paul says have no anxiety at all. That might sound impossible but there are so many things that cause us anxiety, which we can do nothing about and we have to leave in God's hands.

If self pity, guilt, unforgiveness, anger, resentment, fear, and worry work against our having joy, then what will lead to joy? We must decide to be joyful. Paul tells the Philippians "rejoice" as if it is something for them to choose to do rather than it being something that just happens to them. I think it was Abraham Lincoln who said most people are about as happy as they make up their minds to be. Dr. Hans Selye, the scientist who developed and researched the concept of stress, would agree. He said: it's generally not the things outside of us that create stress for us, but it's the way we respond to these things. Next we need to be good and to do good. Otherwise we won't feel good about ourselves. The people in today's gospel ask the Baptist, "what should we do?" John gave them a few specific ideas. All we have to do is read the gospels or the 10 Commandments and we'll get the idea that there's more to a good life than just to say, "I believe!" Lastly, I think gratitude is the final key to unlock the way to joy. And again, being grateful is an intentional thing, it is an attitude we must develop. St. Paul said: "in everything, by prayer and petition, with thanksgiving, make your requests known to God." A heart that is ungrateful is not happy. This is not all that could be said about joy, but it's probably enough for us to think about today.

My closing words for today are don't make yourselves so anxious this season that you lose the joy that can be found only in knowing Jesus' love. "The Lord, your God, is in your midst."

4th Sunday Advent
December 24, 2006

INTRODUCTION – (Mic 5:1-4a; Heb 10:5-10; Luke 1:39-45) The capital of Assyria was in what is today, northern Iraq. The Assyrian army was powerful and was famous for its savagery. They had destroyed the northern kingdom of Israel and did considerable damage to the southern kingdom. They surrounded Jerusalem and were calling for its surrender. Naturally the citizens of Jerusalem were terrified. We hear in today's first reading words of hope spoken to God's people by the prophet Micah. The book of the prophet Micah is very short and this is the only time in three years we hear from him. He promises salvation would come out of an unimportant little village about seven miles south of Jerusalem, the birthplace of King David: Bethlehem. This savior would rescue God's people and lead them to peace.

HOMILY – Soon we will begin our celebration of the birth of our savior, Jesus Christ. The liturgy today invites us to set aside for an hour from all our busyness and to experience with Mary the wonder of God's coming to us.

Today's gospel of the visitation is preceded by the story of the annunciation. The angel Gabriel who asked Mary if she would be the mother of our Savior also informed her that her aged cousin Elizabeth, after years of wanting to have a child, was finally going to have one. "In haste" Mary left Nazareth and made the trip of about 65 or 70 miles (probably a four day trip for her) to the home of Elizabeth and Zechariah near Jerusalem. No doubt the youthful Mary was a big help to her cousin in the three months she stayed with her.

To any observer, here was a young girl coming to help out her relative who was six months pregnant. But the Holy Spirit revealed to Elizabeth what was unable to be seen: Mary was carrying within herself the long awaited savior of God's people. God comes to us in simple, ordinary ways, ways our eyes cannot see but in ways that can be seen through faith and the Holy Spirit. Elizabeth wonders how she should be so honored with a visit from Mary and Jesus. We must ask the same question. How is it we should be so honored that Christ has come into our lives, that he speaks to us through the Scriptures, that he feeds us with his own flesh and blood in the Eucharist, that he hears us when we pray (even if he doesn't always do what we want), that the touches us through the kindness of another.

Sometimes I hear the argument from those who support abortion that we don't know when the human soul comes into a fetus. Jesus could have been only a few days old, for the gospel tells us Mary went to Elizabeth "with haste" after the annunciation. John the Baptist, still unborn, and Elizabeth recognized Mary was carrying within herself something infinitely more than just a blob of tissue. They recognized the wonderful presence of the Son of God and they were filled with joy.

The whole passage is bursting with joy. Elizabeth was excited by Mary's visit. John the Baptist, three months from being born was jumping for joy. The Church has taught that at that moment John was set free from original sin and filled with God's grace. Christ came to him before he was born, he was as it were, baptized or christened. Generally the Church celebrates the feast day of a saint only on their date of death, because that's the day they are born into eternal life. But there are only three holy people whose birthday the Church celebrates, Jesus, Mary and John the Baptist, because they were already in God's grace when they were born. But as Christ came to John before his birth, Christ came to each of us on the day we were reborn through the sacrament of baptism. That should cause all of us to jump for joy, knowing that Christ has come to us, that he has given us his grace and has chosen us to be children of God.

Elizabeth said to Mary "Blessed are you who believed that what was spoken to you by the Lord would be fulfilled." The Greek word used here for "blessed" also means "happy." Mary was happy because she truly believed what the Lord had spoken to her and if you get out your bibles and read what follows today's gospel passage, you will see how truly happy she was. She sang a beautiful hymn of praise to God, a hymn known as the Magnificat. It is this song of praise that we will use for our offertory hymn. Do we really want to be happy? This is the key, do not doubt God, do not doubt his love, do not doubt his presence, do not doubt his teachings. He doesn't always do things the way we think he should, and we don't always know what he thinking. That's why we just have to trust him. Mary didn't always know either what he was up to, but she trusted him always and was always ready to say as her son would in his own life "Behold, I come to do your will, O God."

In a short time we will celebrate the birth of Mary's son. May we always feel the joy that his birth can give us, the assurance that in Jesus God is with us and God loves us. Amen.

Christmas
December 25, 2007

HOMILY – A tune to shop by: Angels we have heard on high; sing so sweetly while we buy. Demons, too, who lobby hard; for maxing out our credit card.

Christmas is a time when kids tell Santa what they want and adults pay for it. Deficits are when adults tell the government what they want and their kids pay for it.

Christmas - we've heard the story many times, yet it continues to touch our hearts. For children though it is especially moving because they are beginning to get a sense of what it's all about for the very first time. We can look at the statues and let our imagination make it all real for us, the joy at the birth of a child, a very special child, the proclamation of this birth from the angels to the shepherds, the poverty of having to be born in a place where animals were kept and having only a bed of straw to lay on, the love of Joseph and Mary for each other and for this child who came to them and to us as a gift from God.

This year I came across a lengthy poem by Ogden Nash called The Christmas That Almost Wasn't. He begins his story telling us about a peaceful kingdom ruled by a wise and gentle king. But he had a nephew who was an evil man. His name just happened to be Evilard. Evilard was an unhappy person and he hated anyone who was happy. Most of all he hated Christmas. One day he gathered some other people just as miserable as he was and he was able to capture the king while the king was taking his nap and he locked the king in the dungeon. Evilard and his gang took over the kingdom and worked to make everyone miserable. One of the first things he did was declare: "There shall be no more Christmas." Evilard decreed: "The man who cries, 'Good Christmas Day!' whall have his gizzard cut away; whoever trims a Christmas tree suspended by the thumbs shall be, and he who sings a jolly carol shall be rolled on spikes inside a barrel..." So spoke the rulers, and grimly smiled thus to destroy one tiny Child, the Christ Child and His Christmas. All the citizens were so upset they couldn't function. Even nature was disturbed. I liked the way Ogden Nash described it: "No one knew when to work, nor yet when to play. For the sun shone by night and the moon shone by day! The mice, they had kittens; the cats, they had puppies; the lions had lambs; and the whales, they had guppies! The ink, it turned white; the mild, it turned black; the pig sang Tweet-tweet, and the cow went Quack-quack. The royal red roses made people to stare, with their flowers in the earth and their roots in the air! The wheat was unground into wheat at the mill, for the river turned round and flowed back up the hill. The spots on the leopard went rolling away and were captured for marbles by urchins at play. Great fires in the towns grew worser and worser; flames put out the firemen instead of vice versa. From headland to mainland, from mainland to isthmus the wide world rebelled 'gainst a world with no Christmas."

I like the way the poems tells us everything in the world was mixed up without Christmas and that's mainly what I want to talk about. Just to complete the poem, however, Christmas was saved by a young shepherd boy with help from St. Wenceslaus. I'm not going to give you the details of how this happened. It would take too long. You'll have to find the book and read it yourself.

The lines of the poem I read tell us the world would be really mixed up if Christ had not been born. We might still be trying to serve hundreds of gods, idols made of gold or silver or wood or stone. We might still be offering people up in human sacrifice to these idols. Would we have ever heard about a loving God, a forgiving God? Would we know that love of God and neighbor are the greatest commandments? Would we have any hope of life after this life, especially risen life? The world would be significantly different, considering over two billion people in the world today believe in Jesus Christ. That's about one third of the world's population. Those who believe in Christ are not perfect. We all sin, we all make mistakes. The peace Christ came to bring us is not here yet. The world is still a better place and we are better people to the extent that we live in his light. Imagine what the world could be if all the different groups of Christians got along with one another and lived Jesus' teachings more seriously. May we continue to live in his grace as we celebrate this great feast of his love. May we look forward to enjoying his love throughout eternity. Amen.

Christmas
December 25, 2006

HOMILY — (Isa 52:7-10; Heb 1:1-6; John 1:1-18) Christmas touches what is most beautiful in our lives and in our faith. Christmas shows us that God wants to be close to us and wants us to be close to him. Christmas tells us God loves us enough that he is willing to share in our poverty and in our suffering. The place where he was born, Bethlehem, which means house of bread, and the manger in which he lay, which was a food trough for animals, reveal to us that he came to be our food, to nourish us with his truth and his light and his love. His birth shows us he came for all people, from the lowly shepherds who were practically the most unimportant people in society to the wise men who came from far away. Every child who is conceived is a sign of hope both to its parents and to the world - who knows what each little life might accomplish. Jesus' coming into our world brings with it the greatest hope of all, hope that we shall live forever in his kingdom.

Today I would like you to use your imagination. Picture what might happen if the statues in our crib were to come alive. What they might say. What they might do. What would Mary tell us? Would she complain of the long trip to Bethlehem bouncing along on the back of a donkey or the inconvenience of not finding a place to stay for the night? Or is it possible that none of that would matter because of the joy she felt at the birth of Jesus. Not only was he her precious child but the angel had told her he would be called holy, Son of God and king forever? Would she, in her love, be covering his little face with her kisses? And Joseph? He really cared about Mary and Jesus. Would he worry about them having to spend the night in a stable? But he was trusting, too, and he may have felt very peaceful knowing he did all he could and God would take care of the rest. What might the shepherds have to tell us? Were they amazed that God chose to tell them, as unimportant as they were, this exciting news that their Messiah and Lord had just been born and he was only a few steps away from them? Did the wise men already see the star and start getting their bags packed so they could go to meet this newly arrived king? The animals, if they could talk, would probably ask, "What's going on with all these people coming and going?" Could they sense the excitement around them and know that they were looking upon their God and Creator? I wonder what Jesus might have said if he could have talked, but he didn't know how to talk yet. He was just born. The divine side of him might have been thinking why did I ever do this. Or his divine side, filled with divine joy from all eternity, might have been feeling joy now as a human infant, ready to bring life and light, healing and salvation to all who would be receptive to his great love. It's interesting to speculate what each person in the stable might have been thinking, feeling, doing, or what they might say to us if they were to come alive.

I want to carry that thought just a little further. If these lifeless statues that remind us of the glorious event of Jesus' birth were to come alive, that would be a stupendous miracle. It's not in the nature of things that a lifeless object suddenly springs to life, and living things that have life do not suddenly take on a higher form of life. Seeds might turn into flowers and tadpoles might turn into frogs, but flowers don't turn into cats and frogs don't turn into whales. Trees do not become squirrels, goldfish do not become horses and rabbits do not become human. I have no quarrel with the idea of evolution if God decided to create higher and more complex forms of life from lower forms of life over thousands of years, but there is considerable consistency and stability in creation. And here is where part of the miracle of Christmas lies. The Son of God came down to us to lift us up, to give us a higher form of life, to make us humans divine. We do not stop being human, but we become much more, we become God's sons and daughters. But we have to open our hearts to him for this to happen. That's why we celebrate Christmas. It's not that the Son of God became bored up in heaven and decided he wanted something different to do, so he decided to come and visit this planet. No! He came to us because he wanted to share with us all the joy and love and life he shared with his Father and with the Holy Spirit from all eternity.

If Jesus, Mary, and Joseph were to say anything to us they would tell us to trust Jesus, to open our hearts to him and to follow his way of love, to love God with our whole selves and to love our neighbor as ourselves. If we do that, everything else will fall into place and we will enjoy eternal happiness. Amen

Feast of the Holy Family
December 31, 2006

HOMILY – (Sir 3:3-7, 14-17a; Col 3:12-21; Matt 2:13-15, 19-23) Psychologists have isolated about a dozen or so characteristics that happy and successful families share, while most unhappy families are unhappy or dysfunctional in their own unique and individual way. I want to talk about only one quality that helps marriages and families to be successful and happy and that is holiness since this is the feast of the Holy Family. This does not mean that holy families are isolated from the ordinary problems of daily life. Holy people have as many problems to deal with in daily life as anyone else, but they have a good support system to fall back on: God, who helps them deal with difficulties. The holy family had their share of problems. If you read the early chapters of St. Matthew and St. Luke's gospels you might get the impression their lives were full of problems. Today's gospel is the only gospel that tells us anything about Jesus as he was growing up. What panic Joseph and Mary must have felt not being able to find him for three days. Every family has good and bad times.

The holy family was holy because God's will was first in their lives. And St. Luke wants us to know this. He pointed out many instances where Mary and Joseph always did what God wanted of them, whether through the message of an angel or by their fidelity to the Jewish law. For example, Luke tells us in today's gospel the holy family would go to the Temple every year to celebrate the feast of Passover. That trip from Galilee to Jerusalem was not like taking a drive to Dayton or Lexington on a Sunday afternoon. Even though Jerusalem was only about 70 miles from Galilee, it would have taken a few days; most people had to travel on foot because they didn't have any other means of transportation and they had to travel in groups too, because travel was dangerous. They could have met robbers or wild animals along the way.

This willingness to do what God wants brings with it the development of many values such as honesty, fidelity, responsibility, and virtues such as Paul mentions in today's second reading: heartfelt compassion, kindness, humility, gentleness, patience, forgiving one another and putting up with one another and above all love which binds them all together and makes them perfect. These values and virtues help people have good relationships. When I say if we are a holy family our family will more likely be happy and successful, I'm not just making up things or proposing theories that I believe are good ideas. A number of statistical studies have shown that regular church goers live happier and more successful lives and have happier and more successful marriages. A few years ago the rate of divorce, for example, was twice as high among non-church goers as it was among church goers.

As we speak of families, I want to say a word about our parish family. Here I use the word family analogously. But I thought I would make some connection with family and parish because this Friday was the 15th anniversary of our merger with St. Patrick's and the 15th anniversary of my appointment to St. Boniface as pastor. Archdiocesan policy is that if a priest is over 65 years of age, he can stay where he is as long as he has the health and energy to do the job. I told the Archbishop I would like to stay here. I won't beat Monsignor Schwartz' record, but, God willing and with good health, I should be good until I'm 75 which will be another six years, then I'll see whether I should stay longer or whether I should retire. My hope is that someone else will step forward to take St. Joseph's Church at the end of June. It's been really hard trying to take care of two parishes. St. Boniface resembles a family in several ways. I feel like a father to so many, having supported and guided many people through hard times throughout the years. Now that I have two parishes, I miss having as much time as I used to have for personal contact with our parishioners here. I enjoy praying at Mass with our parishioners and it pains me when I know people who should be here every week and who seldom are. I would like to hear more people praying and singing. St. Paul tells us, "Let the word of Christ dwell in you richly, as in all wisdom you teach and admonish one another, singing psalms, hymns, and spiritual songs with gratitude in your hearts to God." That's one thing I have to say about St. Joseph's Church. Their responses and singing are spirited. As "father" here in this family I am grateful for all the support I get, moral support, support when we need volunteers, and financial support. Just two weeks ago, for example, I put something in the bulletin about needing to do some repairs on the organ. I made no special pitch or appeal and already we received almost $9,000. One of the things I find most refreshing here is that the people treat me as if I know something. Not that everyone thinks I'm always right, but in other places I've been it felt as if the people thought I didn't know anything and I was there not to be their spiritual leader, but to do whatever they wanted me to do. The only problem with that was everyone had conflicting ideas about what they wanted or what would be helpful to them. As your father, as your pastor, as your spiritual leader, I want to say I'm glad to be part of this spiritual family where I see genuine holiness and love.

Going back to my main theme of family, do you want to be a healthy family? If you can keep two rules uppermost in your family relationships (keep God first and love one another), you have most of the battle won.

Mary, Mother of God
January 1, 2007

HOMILY – (Num 6:22-27; Gal 4:4-7; Luke 2:16-21) Today we begin a new year. It's been a difficult year in many ways. Yet we celebrate. Why? Perhaps because 2006 is over. Perhaps because we've made it this far in spite of problems and dangers. Hopefully, we celebrate also in gratitude for the good things that happened. And finally I think we celebrate because we are essentially optimistic people. We have hope in the future in spite of possible dangers and inevitable problems. Optimism is the only attitude a Christian can adopt because we believe in the goodness of God and his plans for our eternal happiness. St. Paul's statement in Romans has always been a source of strength and optimism for me: "For those who love God, all things work out for good." (Rom. 8, 28) If I didn't believe that, I would be very depressed. Our optimism is grounded in reality, however, and we can be sure the coming year will not be wonderful in every way. So we begin the year with prayer, the greatest prayer we have, the Mass, asking for God's blessing and help for the future.

My friends suggested I make my remarks short and sweet; no one will feel like listening to anything too heavy or too lengthy today, they assured me. Well, I will be short, but the beginning of a new year is a profound event. And so I want to offer two ideas that are extremely important.

The first concerns how we answer the most profound questions about the meaning of life, the meaning of our own life and where our life is taking us. Popular culture, TV talk shows, the people we hang around with, the books we read, the variety of religious beliefs in the world today all give us ideas as to why we're here and where we're going. Everything we do this year will be fundamentally guided by the answers we give to these questions. Even to make no decision about these basic life issues is to make a decision. Our faith tells us there is only one reliable answer: the teachings of our Lord Jesus Christ. Jesus is God's Son who came to earth to show us the way to eternal life. "I am the way, the truth and the life," he tells us. Any other way will lead us nowhere. That's why we pray, why we come to Mass, why we are encouraged to read the Scriptures, so we can be guided by his light, his wisdom, his truth.

My second profound thought is about time. It is precious. Use it well. And if we haven't used it well in the past, it's not too late to start over. Amen.

Feast of the Epiphany
January 7, 2007

INTRODUCTION – (Isa 60:1-6; Eph 3:2-3a, 5-6; Matt 2:1-12) 587 years before Christ, God's people were conquered and enslaved by the Babylonians and taken to Babylon, the area around modern day Baghdad. Fifty years later the Persians, the people who lived in what is today Iran, conquered the Babylonians and they allowed the Jews to return to their homeland. In our first reading the prophet enthusiastically proclaims this return: "Rise up in splendor, Jerusalem! Your light has come..." The prophet, however, sees in this event something much more wonderful than the Jews' return from captivity. He sees Jerusalem becoming the center of spirituality and light for all the world. People would come from all over to visit Jerusalem and to be nourished by the spiritual light and life radiating from it. This vision of the prophet begins to be fulfilled in Jesus' death and resurrection in Jerusalem. From there his light spreads out to all the world. As described so beautifully in the book of Revelation, those who follow Christ's light will enter into a new and eternal Jerusalem.

HOMILY – Today, the feast of the Epiphany, is the original feast of Jesus' birth. Eastern Christians were celebrating the birth of Jesus on January 6th years before Christians in Rome began to celebrate the birth of Jesus on December 25th. Because Epiphany was already well established as a major feast by the time the Roman Church started celebrating the birth of Jesus on December 25th, the Roman Church could not ignore it, so they centered on the coming of the magi as the theme for the feast of the Epiphany. This extended the Christmas celebration for a number of days, which is appropriate, because Christmas is too wonderful an event to limit to only one day.

The word Epiphany comes from a Greek word which means coming to light or appearing. The shepherds who lived in the area of Bethlehem had already had their epiphany when the angels announced the birth of Jesus to them. Today we commemorate God's revelation of the coming of his Son to magi. Magi is a term that designated persons who were priests of a pagan cult and were experts in astrology, interpretation of dreams and various other occult arts. Their primary job would be to act as advisors to the rulers of the people of Persia (ancient people who lived in modern day Iran). As advisors to the king and his court they would have studied the stars for messages from the gods. As pagans they remind us that Christ's saving light is meant for people of every race and every nationality.

If we understand the word Epiphany as a general word indicating God revealing himself to anyone, then Epiphany does not end with the visit of the magi. God continues to reveal himself to all people. Some people respond to the revelation and some do not.

That is the point St. Matthew is making for us in today's gospel. The magi searched for Christ and found him. The same opportunities to find our Lord were available to Herod and the Jewish high priests, but they didn't find him, either because they were uninterested or they had hostile intent. Herod wanted to find him in order to kill him and the high priests, although they knew where the Messiah was to be born, couldn't be bothered going there themselves to look for him. Christ can be found by anyone whose intent to find him is honest and who doesn't give up the search. Christ wants us to know him, that's why he came to us and he came a long way to make it possible for us to find him. We have to go part of the way too. He will not disappoint us if we really want to know him. May God's Spirit fill us with light so we can continually find him in new and deeper ways.

Baptism of the Lord
January 8, 2007

INTRODUCTION – (Isa 42:1-4, 6-7; Acts 10:34-38; Matt 3:13-17) Today's first reading is closely connected with Jesus' baptism. This first reading was written over 500 years before Christ. It is a mysterious passage in that scholars do not know who the prophet was writing about. But in hindsight, we can see how perfectly Jesus fulfilled this description of God's servant. The words that introduce our first reading are directly connected with the account of Jesus' baptism. In our first reading God introduces his servant in this way: "Here is my servant whom I uphold, my chosen one with whom I am well pleased." And it is on this servant that God has put his spirit. God's words at Jesus' baptism are almost exactly the same except for one word that is changed. At Jesus' baptism, God speaks of Jesus as his Son. And upon Jesus God the Father sends the Spirit. We have here something more than just an introduction of God's Son to the world and his being empowered by the Spirit. The words of the Father also gave direction to Jesus' future work. Jesus was being called for the victory of justice. He was to be a covenant of the people, a light for the nations as described in this servant passage from Isaiah.

HOMILY – The baptism of John the Baptist was a baptism of repentance. Jesus was God's Son, human like us in every way, except he was without sin. Why would he present himself for baptism by John? If you are confused about the baptism of Jesus you are in good company.   The early Church was confused and somewhat uncomfortable about it. St. Matthew reports John saying to Jesus "I ought to be baptized by you, yet you come to me." St. Luke, as we heard in today's gospel, hardly mentions the baptism itself. And St. John in his gospel makes only an indirect reference to it. Yet all the gospels as well as the Acts of the Apostles know that it happened, but they struggled to understand it.

Jesus did not have sin to repent of, so John's baptism had no relevance in this regard. One approach to understanding this event is to see it as a clarification of who Jesus is. He is God's Son, his beloved, with whom the Father is well pleased. There would be no question about Jesus' identity. Jesus' identity had already been revealed to us in Luke's gospel when the angel told Mary at the annunciation that she would conceive her child through the power of the Holy Spirit and he would be holy and would be called Son of God. Jesus' identity was also revealed when Jesus was lost in the temple for three days and when he was found he said to his parents: "why were you looking for me? Didn't you know I must be in my Father's house?" But his identity was hidden from everyone around them. It was only when Jesus was baptized and God announced to the world "This is my beloved Son" and the Spirit came down upon him that the world was to know who he was.

Our baptism gives us our identity too. It tells us: we are God's child, sharing God's life, beloved by the Father and called to live our lives in a way that is pleasing to our heavenly Father. So often we forget who we are and that we are God's beloved. The advertising media is constantly telling us we don't measure up, we're not worthwhile. We're not as beautiful, as shapely, as energetic, as stylish, as popular, as successful, as wonderful, as happy as we should be. But do not despair! The ads tell us the product they happen to be promoting will make everything better. It will solve our problems and make us over into someone worthwhile.

God has already made us someone worthwhile. He first made us in his image and likeness. More than that he has given us his life. He has made us his beloved son or daughter. Archbishop Tutu, the Anglican bishop from South Africa, says he always preaches one message to his people there. His message is simple and he repeats it over and over again. It is that "God loves you." "I tell them that," he says, "because the entire culture tells them that they are unlovable, and I have to give them the message of who they really are, because God loves them."

Through baptism we have been defined forever as God's children and the only one who can deface or destroy that dignity that has been given to us is we, ourselves.

But, Jesus' baptism not only clarified for all the world who Jesus was, but it also gave Jesus his mission. He was to be a covenant of the people and a light for the nations. Especially he was called to establish justice on the earth. Justice here means "righteousness," fidelity to God, goodness, living up to what we know God wants of us. Who we are should define how we live. If a person is a policeman, he or she is to work to uphold the law. If a person is a doctor, he or she has a concern about people's health. If a person is a teacher, he or she is oriented toward helping people grow in wisdom and knowledge. If we are God's child, we are called to live up to that dignity. And in trying to live up to that dignity, who better could we imitate than the perfect Son of God, with whom the Father was well pleased.

As we celebrate Jesus' baptism, may we at the same time celebrate our own. May we rejoice in God's gift of love and life given to us, and may we live up to the high dignity with which God has blessed us.

2nd Sunday of Ordinary Time
January 14, 2007

INTRODUCTION – (Isa 62:1-5; 1 Cor 12:4-11; John 2:1-11) Five hundred thirty years before Christ the Jews were exiles in Babylon. You've heard me mention this many, many times. Today's first reading is an announcement from the prophet that the Persians, who had conquered the Babylonians, were going to let God's people go home. Their cities and homes were in ruins during the time of their exile and the Persians were even willing to give them some material help to rebuild. God said he would forgive the sins of his people, their sins that brought on their exile, and God would take them back. God would make Jerusalem and Judea his spouse. The image of God marrying his people is an important biblical image and is the best symbol from our human experience that can be used to describe the love and intimacy God desires to have with his people. The image prepares the way for gospel account of the marriage feast of Cana.

HOMILY – I want to encourage you to make sure you have truly invited Christ into your homes and into your relationships, especially your marriage relationship if you are married.

Several years ago I read the story about a couple who bought a new home and spent a lot of money on interior decoration. The wife, who wrote the article, had a husband who wanted to hang a large picture of the Sacred Heart in a prominent place in their living room and the lady objected. It did not fit with the décor of their new home. But he insisted and reminded her of Jesus' words: "Everyone who acknowledges me before others I will acknowledge before my heavenly Father." (Mt. 10,32) Being a religious person, she gave in to his wishes and hung the picture. In her article she told about a few incidents that happened because the picture was there. One visitor, who kept glancing at the picture, eventually commented that "Jesus doesn't look at you, he looks right through you." Another friend commented, "I always feel so peaceful in your home." She said one of the most striking things she noticed was that inevitably the conversation with friends and relatives was drawn to a higher plane. She felt overall the picture had a good effect on their family. Her article concluded with the statement: "This much I know, when you invite Jesus into your home, you are never the same again."

I'm sure the couple in today's gospel would agree. Wedding receptions were major celebrations in the culture and time of Jesus. They went on for several days and planning for one would have been difficult, but running out of wine would have been a long remembered embarrassment for the bride and groom. So Jesus came to their rescue, with a little prompting from his mother. And he rescued them big time.

Others we hear about in the gospel had their lives changed significantly for the better by inviting Jesus into their home. Peter brought Jesus to his home and Jesus healed his mother-in-law. A little girl died who was the daughter of a synagogue official named Jairus. Jairus went to find Jesus and Jesus came to his home and raised his daughter to life. He healed a man of dropsy one evening while having dinner at the home of a leading Pharisee. He became good friends with Martha, Mary and Lazarus and visited them when he came to

Jerusalem. When Lazarus died Jesus brought him back to life. This is not to mention how people's lives were changed in other ways because they opened their doors to Jesus.

Certainly, inviting Jesus into our lives begins by opening our hearts to him. But what if we lived in a country where it is illegal to be a Christian and the police came to our home, would there be enough evidence there to convict us? Do we have religious books or periodicals, any religious articles that remind us of our Lord or Mary or one of the saints, is there a bible somewhere within reach or is it on a shelf covered with dust? If our houses were bugged by the police, would we ever get caught praying with other family members?

When Jesus sent his disciples out he always told them to say "Peace to this house" whenever they entered a house. It is his desire to bring peace wherever he goes. In the book of Revelation Jesus makes this promise to us: "Behold, I stand at the door and knock. If anyone hears my voice and opens the door, (then) I will enter his house and dine with him, and he with me." He will not invade our space. He wants to be invited in.

That goes doubly in marriage. St. John tells us "God is love." If people want love in their marriage, they need to have God as the foundation of their relationship. I always have major concerns about couples who call up and want to have their marriage at St. Boniface, but they've not been going to Church. They are missing the essential ingredient for a loving and successful life ahead. I always challenge them that if they want me to have their wedding, then I want to see them become serious enough about their faith that they start practicing it.

St. John tells us today this was the first of Jesus' signs. As a sign it shows Jesus' high regard for marriage. But it shows much more. It tells us Jesus was interested in more than just keeping the party going, that he came to bring abundant blessings to those who believe in him. Today he works greater miracle for us by changing bread and wine into his own body and blood. May we be filled with his love as we receive the food and drink he gives us. Amen.

Third Sunday in Ordinary Time
January 21, 2007

INTRODUCTION – (Neh 8:2-4a, 5-6, 8-10; 1 Cor 12:12-30; Luke 1:1-4; 4:14-21) You've heard frequently of the Babylonian exile and how the Persians conquered the Babylonians fifty years later and allowed the Jews to return home. Many of the Jews in Babylon had become rather comfortable there and they did not return to Israel all at once. Little by little they came. Even a hundred years after they began to return they were still struggling to rebuild their cities and their civilization. The Persians were still in control of the entire Middle East which included Israel. Nehemiah, a Jew, had been a high level servant to the king of Persia and he asked his king to allow him to return to Israel to help his people rebuild. So the king of Persia appointed him to be governor of Israel. In Nehemiah's efforts to rebuild the nation, he had to start with what was most important and that was to remind the people that God had to take first place in their lives. He realized much of the trauma his people had gone through at the time of their exile was because they had forgotten their God. In today's first reading Nehemiah called for a general assembly of the people and the priest Ezra read God's word to them. Remember, ordinary people did not have books in those days. Books were very rare and very expensive, since each one had to be individually written word by word. So, if the ordinary person were ever to know God's word, someone had to read it or preach it to them. Ezra, thus, read God's word to the people and interpreted it for them. The reading was most probably from the first five books of the bible. Notice that there was active participation on the part of God's people as they heard the word, possibly for the first time: raising their hands, answering "amen," bowing to the ground, listening attentively, weeping and rejoicing.

HOMILY – The central theme of today's liturgy is God's word. The people were saddened by God's word in today's first reading. Perhaps they recognized how they had failed to live up to it. But Ezra and Nehemiah told the people God's word should bring us joy. Even if they had not been living by God's word, on hearing it they could learn from it and start living as God instructed them. When we break the laws of our society, we may get thrown into jail. God doesn't send the police around when we break his laws, but when we ignore his word, it's going to catch up with us in the long run. So many people rationalize bad behavior by saying Jesus is a good guy. He won't punish me for this or that. But they forget, Jesus didn't come to punish us. He came to show us the way to happiness and eternal life. When we choose a way contrary to his teaching we bring unhappiness upon ourselves.

One of my favorite psalm verses is: "Your word is a lamp for my steps and a light for my path." (Ps 119, 105) If you have to go somewhere in the dark, it's nice to have a flashlight to help you see where you're going. You can walk in the dark if you wish, but that would not be very smart and you might be likely to end up hurting yourself. When we try to make it through life without God's word, we're walking in the dark. We can't say God is punishing us if, while we're walking in the dark, we run into something or we fall. We did it to ourselves.

Nehemiah knew the people needed God's light if they were ever going to succeed in getting back on their feet. Jesus knows we need God's light. In today's gospel, Jesus is beginning his public ministry and he uses the Scriptures to describe the work he will do. People were impressed at first, but unfortunately, as we will hear next week, they rejected him.

Jesus said "Today this Scripture passage is fulfilled in your hearing." "Today" is the important word here. It tells us God is speaking to us whenever we hear the Scriptures. Those who heard Ezra read the word of God and interpret it were hearing about things that happened almost a thousand years before, the stories of Abraham, Moses and the Exodus. But they saw its relevance for them that day. Jesus read from the book of Isaiah, written centuries before he was born, but he told his audience it had great meaning for them that day. "Today this Scripture passage is fulfilled in your hearing." God's word always speaks to us because God is a living God and his Spirit continues to communicate to us through that word.

In our second reading today, Paul reminds us of the importance of community. He tells us we can't say I don't need a church, I don't need to come to Mass, I don't need to pray with all those other people. We do need to because we are part of the body of Christ and we can't say we do not need one another. When we separate ourselves from one another, we are denying the spiritual gifts God has given to others to help us and we are denying to others the spiritual gifts God has given us to help them. We need each other. We need to share our faith with each other, even if it is a matter of praying with one another. To sum everything up, we need God's word and we need each other to make it through this life to the joys of eternal life.

Fourth Sunday in Ordinary Time
January 28, 2007

INTRODUCTION – (Jer 1:4-5, 17-19; 1 Cor 12:31-13:13; Luke 4:21-30) Matthew, Mark and Luke begin to tell us about Jesus' public ministry with the baptism of John the Baptist. They tell us nothing about what happened during those thirty years between his birth and his baptism except for the one instance when Jesus' parents lost him in the Temple at the age of twelve. I suspect Jesus lived a fairly ordinary life, working in the trade of his foster father, Joseph, as was the custom in those days. After Jesus baptism and his 40 days of trial and testing in the desert, they all move on to tell us about Jesus' public ministry in slightly different ways. St. Luke describes how Jesus began his public ministry with a visit to his hometown, Nazareth. In several places in his gospel, Luke tells us Jesus and his parents were devout Jews and faithfully followed God' laws. We would expect no less. Luke tells us it was Jesus' custom to go to the synagogue every Sabbath. He was invited to give a reading from the Scriptures and he chose Isaiah. Then he began to comment on what he read and his comments were well received. We heard all of this in last Sunday's gospel. Today the story continues. We don't know specifically what happened, but what began as a good experience turned out very badly. His former friends and neighbors were basically asking, "Who does he think he is? Where did he get the authority to teach us?" Within a short time they attempted to throw him off a cliff. We don't know how he escaped their murderous intentions, but he did. Our first reading, as usual, prepares us for the gospel. Jeremiah the prophet heard God's call to preach God's word, a calling that would lead to suffering and rejection.

HOMILY – Calvin Coolidge, who was a man of few words, came home from church one day and his wife asked him what the preacher talked about. He said "Sin." She asked, "What did he say about it?" He said "He was against it!" If someone asks you what the preacher talked about today you can say "Just ordinary stuff!" "Ordinary" is the keyword of my remarks today. I think one of the reasons Jesus got into trouble in Nazareth was because he was so ordinary. His friends and neighbors could not conceive that he was any better than they were. St. Luke glosses over the conflict between Jesus and his neighbors with the one question he tells us they asked: "Isn't this the son of Joseph?" But if you read St. Mark's account of Jesus visit to Nazareth, Mark is very blunt. He tells us the people were asking "Where did this man get all this? What is this wisdom that has been given him? Isn't this the carpenter, the son of Mary...?" In that culture boys were identified by their father. Calling Jesus the son of Mary is an allusion to Joseph not being Jesus' natural father and would have been an insult both to Mary and Jesus. Their rejection of Jesus and their desire to kill him foreshadow the future of Jesus.

In today's second reading we heard one of the best known and best loved passages in Scripture: St. Paul's description of love. What is so beautiful about this passage is that it doesn't deal with those thrilling moments when all of our being is charged with excitement and joy. It deals with the ordinary, everyday kind of love that ordinary living requires. Paul describes this kind of love by telling us what love is not rather than what it is. It is not jealous, pompous, rude or selfish, it is not short-tempered nor does it hold grudges. It is patient and kind and trusting and willing to put up with all kinds of little annoyances. This is not about falling in love - a period of infatuation that may or may not lead to real love. Paul is talking about our ordinary day-to-day contact with other people, some of whom we may not like a whole lot, but whom we learn how to be kind to nevertheless. Practicing this ordinary kind of love doesn't always sweep us off our feet, but it does bring a kind of joy, because our vocation and our fulfillment in life is to learn how to love one another.

On this fourth Sunday of Ordinary time we hear about ordinary things. But in the ordinary is the extraordinary if we know how to find it. As the poet George Eliot said: "If we had a keen vision of all that is ordinary in human life, it would be like hearing the grass grow or the squirrel's heartbeat, and we should die of that roar which is the other side of silence." It is through ordinary things that God touches our lives most of the time, through prayer and music, through the same Scriptures we've heard again and again, through bread and wine, and through the weekly Eucharist. We are perhaps surrounded by the same ordinary people we've seen week after week for years. Through our being together in prayer we become one body in Christ, and in Christ we love and worship our heavenly Father. Sometimes it feels pretty ordinary, but for those who can see more deeply, the mystery we celebrate is awesome.

Fifth Sunday of Ordinary Time
February 4, 2007

HOMILY – (Isa 6:1-2a, 3-8; 1 Cor 15:1-11; Luke 5:1-11) Our first reading is one of my favorites. It is from the prophet Isaiah who lived about 725 years before Christ. He describes his call from God to be a prophet. The setting is in Jerusalem in the Temple. Notice he is unable to describe what God looked like. He describes God's royal robe, the angels, the sounds and the profound sense of God's holiness. In this experience he becomes aware of his own unworthiness. You will recognize in this passage the inspiration for two familiar hymns: the Holy, Holy which we say or sing at every Mass and the hymn, Here I Am, Lord.

In the other two readings we hear how two other people experienced God in Jesus Christ: Paul in his vision of the Risen Christ and Peter in the miraculous catch of fish.

HOMILY – If we were walking along the street and found a wallet full of money we probably wouldn't say "What luck that all the molecules in the atmosphere just happened to come together right now to produce this money for me to find!" We might like to say that so that we wouldn't have to worry about who might have lost it. But, in spite of the fact that it may have been lucky that we found it, we know that nature doesn't just produce piles of money for people to find. Yet people can look at the planets and stars, the various forms of life on this earth, and many other marvels in this universe that we are still discovering and say "What luck that the molecules floating around this universe somehow came together by accident and produced all of this. Just don't ask where the molecules came from.

Most people prefer to say there was a power greater than we can imagine at work here, a power we call the Creator, the Supreme Being, or simply God. But can we know something more about God than that God is someone greater than we are? That is an important question because some day we hope to be spending a lot of time with God and even in our present everyday lives God can be a source of power and wisdom for us. So that is a very relevant question, how can we get to know God better? What we can figure out on our own is so very limited. It's personal experience that helps us to know more. Many people have claimed to have had personal experiences of God. I'm sure that most of the people here in church have had moments when God's presence became very real to them. Unfortunately those moments are infrequent and usually rather brief.

We see in today's readings that God chose certain individuals who have had special experiences of God and to whom God gave a special mission to teach others about him. Isaiah experienced God in the Temple, most probably while in prayer. After the experience God asked, "Whom shall I send? Who will go for us?" Isaiah answered, "Here I am, send me!" Paul was on his way to arrest people who believed in Jesus when Jesus appeared to him. Through this experience he came to know Jesus as Lord and he experienced that God had chosen him to preach to the nations. Then we heard about Peter who experienced God in Jesus through a miraculous catch of fish. After Jesus gave Peter a catch of fish that astounded even him, the professional fisherman, Jesus said, "From now on you will be catching people."

Our insert in today's bulletin tells us about the Church and how it grew. I like the way the author of the article describes this growth. He said it wasn't gradual, but it was an explosion, revealing the power of the Spirit at work in the apostles and in the early Church. It was not only Isaiah, Paul and Peter who taught us about God but most of all it was Jesus Christ. And saints and scholars have continued to reveal God to us.

There is a tendency among many Christians to take what they like from the gospels and ignore the rest. If we are to know God, we have to listen also to those elements of God's self-revelation that are not so easy to hear. Following only the parts of the gospel we like will not lead us to God any more than reading only the books you enjoy will get you through college or playing a sport without the discipline of practice or hard work will make you an athlete. The journey to God is often easy and pleasant, but sometimes God takes us through dark valleys, steep hills and rugged terrain. But even in hard times he is always there to help us.

Common sense may convince an open minded person that there is a God, but we have to look further to get to know God better. Our own personal experiences can help us, but they are limited too. We have heard today about three spiritual giants who can teach us a lot more. Through meditation and reflection on the teachings and the testimony of prophets, apostles and saints and especially through the revelation of Jesus Christ we can come to know the God of the universe more personally and more fully. Today we gather in faith and prayer, thanking God for what we have come to know through the experiences and testimony of others, and asking him to enrich the faith and knowledge we have. Amen.

6th Sunday of Ordinary Time
February 11, 2007

INTRODUCTION – (Jer 17:5-8; 1 Cor 15:12, 16-20; Luke 6:17, 20-26) Life is full of options for people in the world today, but the Bible tells us that all our options ultimately will be reduced to two. We either make God the center of our lives or we don't. Choosing to make God the center of our lives will lead to true happiness, making any other choice may satisfy us temporarily, but it will in the end leave us disappointed and unhappy. This was crystal clear to Jeremiah the prophet who lived at the time of the Babylonian exile. His way of expressing this truth is crystal clear too.

HOMILY – We are more familiar with St. Matthew's beatitudes. They tend to be more spiritualized than St. Luke's version which we just heard. St. Luke's version is a little more puzzling and perhaps unsettling. The Greek word which is translated here as blessed also means happy. Jesus is saying some of the most unlikely people are happy while the ones you would suppose should be happy are in deep trouble. He is saying happy are you who are poor, you who are hungry, you who are weeping, happy are you when people hate you. He goes on to say it's bad news for those who are rich, the well fed, those who are laughing and having fun and those who are well liked. They face great sorrow and disaster. Pretty strong, isn't it!

Certainly our Lord is not advocating that poverty, hunger, grieving and being rejected by our friends and neighbors is virtuous. As a matter of fact Jesus encouraged people to care for the poor, even to the point of promising eternal reward to those who feed the hungry, give drink to the thirsty, clothe the naked, visit the sick, etc. And he even invited some people to give everything they had to the poor. He also had some friends who had to have been fairly financially well off. He is simply warning us with forceful language, we better not build our happiness on partying, being well off and well liked. Life goes deeper than that and so does our happiness. Like a tree that sinks its roots deep into the earth to receive water and nourishment, we have to have our lives rooted in God, which means obeying the Commandments, taking time for prayer and having an active love for others.

This past Friday I was driving down the expressway from Dayton and as the wind gusts kept pushing my car into the left lane, I had to keep turning the steering wheel to the right just so I could keep going straight ahead. That's what I think our Lord is doing here in St. Luke as he preaches to the people of his day. Like a strong wind, the values of this world keep pushing us to invest fully in the pleasures of this life. Our Lord is trying to pull us back so our lives do not end up in great sorrow and disaster. We face many options in our lives, but in the end only one will really count, whether we have made Christ and his law of love for God and for each other the central value in our life. If we haven't, we will be sorry and it will be too late.

Anthony De Mello in one of his many inspiring books gives us a parable of life to ponder. There were a group of tourists riding in their tour bus. The shades on the windows were pulled down and they were busy arguing about what to watch on TV, who had the cutest outfit, who got to sit where and with whom, where they were going to eat lunch and they were totally unaware that they were passing through beautiful countryside: lakes, mountains, green fields and rivers. Some people go through life and miss the best parts. The human race started out on the wrong foot, looking for happiness in the wrong place and we still do. The God who created us and who knows us best of all is trying to tell us where we will find it.

This week we commemorate, as we do every year, four chaplains who were on a ship that got torpedoed in the Second World War. As the ship was going down, they helped to hand out life jackets to the men on the ship. When they came to the end of their supply, each of them took off their own life jacket and gave it away. They went down with the ship praying together and encouraging each other. They are a beautiful example of Jesus' words, "greater love than this no one has, than that he lay down his life for his friends." (Jn 15, 13). They are also a powerful example of hope in the resurrection and the next life which St. Paul tells us about today.

When we're young this life seems very long, but the longer we live the more aware we become of how short it is. There's another life beyond this one. God wants us to be with him, so he can share his happiness with us. But we have to follow the way he's shown us. Jesus would not have bothered to come to us, to teach us, and to die for us if it didn't matter how we live our life. Too many people in society today adopted a credit card mentality in their spiritual life. You know the credit card mentality: buy now and pay later. About their spiritual life they say "I'm not going to worry about it until pay-off time." I can say that for a variety of reasons that usually doesn't work. If we don't live our faith now, it may not be there to help us at the end of life.

First Sunday of Lent
February 25, 2007

INTRODUCTION – (Deut 26:4-10; Rom 10:8-13; Luke 4:1-13) Any person who has a sense of spirituality knows deep down that we owe our Creator recognition, respect, worship, gratitude and honor. Throughout the history of the human race, honor and recognition were offered in a variety of ways. It was not unusual to find that many primitive tribes offered human sacrifices. God was not honored by this practice, and he revealed this to the Jewish people. Instead they made offerings of the various foods that sustained their lives to indicate they recognized that all they had, including life itself, came from God. In our first reading we hear Moses instructing the people in the proper way to offer their tithes and the first fruits of their land. The reading leads us into the gospel where Jesus tells Satan, and what he tells him is a reminder to all of us, that we owe worship to God only.

HOMILY – This past Wednesday we began the holy season of Lent. The word "Lent" is an Old English word for spring. It's an appropriate word. As the season of spring prepares the earth to break forth into new life, the season of Lent is a time to prepare to break forth, spiritually, into new life. I read that, historically, Lent started out as a time of prayer, fasting and doing good works for those who were preparing to become members of the Church at Easter. These are the people who are going through what we refer to today as the RCIA. Since early Christian communities were quite small (you know they killed people for being Christians then) it would have been an exciting time when a new member was preparing to embrace Christ through baptism. The early Christian communities would join with those preparing for baptism by also making this season a time of prayer, fasting and doing good works. Even though most Church goers today are only remotely conscious of new members joining the Church, it is still fitting that this season continue to be a time to prepare for new life. There may be some among us who are perfect but for most of us, our life in Christ can always benefit from some greater or lesser degree of spiritual renewal. In addition, there is our eternal life we all need to prepare for. In the early Church, those who had sinned seriously and publicly did public penance during this time of Lent. By wearing sackcloth and ashes and by asking for prayers, they could prepare themselves for returning to the community before Easter. This is how Lent took on a penitential aspect. Many people today use this time of Lent to repent of their mistakes of the past. Add to this the example of Jesus who prayed and fasted in preparation for his public ministry, and we can all find some kind of motivation to make this a holy season of prayer, fasting and doing good works.

Many of us grew up viewing Lent as a gloomy time when we had to practice difficult forms of self-discipline. Today there is a more joyful side to Lent if we see it as preparing us for a deeper relationship with God. Preparing for other important things in life sometimes requires hard work and self-discipline. Why should we think our spiritual life should somehow be different? St. Paul doesn't think so. Self-discipline is not a bad thing even if it is sometimes hard. Psychologically a person who lacks self-discipline cannot be a mature or happy person, so it is a good thing to learn.

Our world would be a little better and all of us would be a lot happier if each one of us decided to work harder on making ourselves a better person. As we begin the season of Lent, our Scripture readings at Mass will call us to conversion, to change our hearts, to turn a little, or maybe a lot more into the kind of person we know God wants us to be.

As we move into the last two weeks of Lent, however, we begin to focus on Christ's passion. A few years ago a movie entitled the Passion of the Christ came out. It was very moving and it helped us remember what Christ did for us to save us. We often forget. We often forget how much we owe our Creator. One reason why Sunday is dedicated to offering God worship and praise is so we don't forget. We do not offer animals or other food as the Jews did. Instead, we have the perfect sacrifice. Our participation in the Mass unites us with the perfect act of worship and love and obedience offered to the Father by Jesus as he died on the cross.

Our readings today put things in perspective by reminding us of the worship we owe God, our Creator.

They remind us we need more than material things to truly live and to be fully human: it's not by bread alone that we live. They remind us God must take priority over everything else in our lives for God alone deserves our worship. I pray that everyone here will have a spiritually enriching Lent as we prepare for new and more abundant life in Christ.

Second Sunday of Lent
March 4, 2007

INTRODUCTION – (Gen 15:5-12, 17-18; Phil 3:17–4:1; Luke 9:28b-36) Almost 4000 years ago, God made awesome promises to a man named Abram about how he would inherit much land, would have so many descendants they could not be counted, even how the whole world would be blessed through him. Abram had no evidence that these promises would ever be fulfilled. He asked God for some assurance that they would. So God gave Abram a special sign. It may seem complicated to us but it would have been easily understood by Abram. It was the way people made covenants or contracts in those days. The ritual of cutting an animal in half and walking between the halves was a symbolic way of saying "may the same thing happen to me as to this animal if I am unfaithful to my word." God is often represented as fire, and in this experience only God moved in-between the two halves of the animals. This indicated that God was not asking Abram to promise anything. God asked only for Abram's trust.

HOMILY – As our lives move along, there are disappointments but there are also hopes and promises that we look forward to. Abram (later named Abraham) looked forward to the promise of land, many descendants and numerous blessings. In an ecstatic experience God assured him his hopes would be fulfilled.

Jesus had several times warned his apostles that he would suffer and die. Now he gave three of them a special experience to help them know what was ahead, that his death would lead to glory. It was a glory so wonderful that they didn't want it to stop. They wanted to set up tents on the mountain, not for themselves but for Jesus, Moses and Elijah, and they wanted to stay there indefinitely. But it wasn't to be. They still had to go through challenging and difficult times before they came to the glory they had seen. Matthew and Mark leave us in the dark regarding what Jesus was talking about with Moses and Elijah, but Luke tells us they were talking about Jesus' departure from this world by his death in Jerusalem. That departure is translated here by the word "exodus." Jesus had to leave this world to enter into the glory that was ahead. Luke has thus allowed us to see there is a definite connection between the transfiguration and Jesus' passion. Perhaps the experience of the transfiguration was meant to give strength and hope to Peter, James, and John, to help them survive Jesus' arrest and crucifixion. Perhaps it was a gift from God the Father to Jesus to help bolster his commitment to be faithful to his mission. Whatever it was, it was a promise of future glory and an assurance that God would not let down those who trusted in him.

When Peter wanted to put up three tents for Jesus, Moses and Elijah, it is always understood that he was enjoying this ecstatic experience and didn't want it to end, and this is true. But I wonder whether Peter, in his way of thinking, was making Jesus equal to Moses and Elijah. He said: "Let us make three tents," as if Jesus were a great leader on a par with Moses and Elijah. God the Father's words: "This is my chosen Son" let the apostles know that Moses and Elijah were great men and great prophets, but Jesus is God's Son and no one could ever be on the same level with him.

If the transfiguration is a promise of future glory for Jesus and the Apostles, St. Paul gives us a promise of future glory for us when he tells us today "our citizenship is in heaven." We are only tourists in this world and it's not our true home. We must always have our bags packed because we never know when we will be called to move on. And we will be called. Paul tells us God "will change our lowly bodies to conform with his glorified body." We will be transfigured also. Lent helps us remember to be ready to move on and to make any changes in our lives we need to make, so we will be ready to meet our God in eternal glory.

Mass is always an assurance and a promise of what's ahead, especially in Communion. The consecrated bread and wine are Jesus' body and blood. We are reminded of his death for us. We are also assured that he hasn't left us orphans, but he is still with us and in Communion he wants us to be more closely united with himself. Someday we will enjoy perfect union when we will not have to experience him through signs and sacraments. We will know him directly and intimately. When we come to that stage, like the three apostles at the transfiguration, we won't ever want to leave. Unlike the apostles, we won't have to.

Third Sunday of Lent
March 11, 2007

INTRODUCTION – (Exod 3:1-8a, 13-15; 1 Cor 10:1-6, 10-12; Luke 13:1-9) Our psalm refrain, "The Lord is kind and merciful," describes our theme for today.

We hear about God's desire to bring his people, suffering as slaves in Egypt, into freedom. He chooses Moses to be the one to demand and obtain their freedom. Moses wasn't happy to have to do this. He had escaped from Egypt himself because he had killed an Egyptian who had attacked an Israelite. Now God tells him he has to go back and deal with the Egyptian king. God gives Moses a special gift, God's name: "Yahweh," translated as "I AM." What is so special about that? It was like giving someone your private phone number. God was assuring Moses of a special relationship Moses would have with him and letting Moses know he could call on God whenever he needed him.

In our second reading Paul reminds us of how many blessings and marvels God's people experienced as God led them through the desert to the Promised Land. But in spite of all the wonderful things God gave them, they were unable to enter into the Promised Land. In the end they had failed to continue trusting in God. He tells us not to be like them.

The theme that "the Lord is kind and merciful" shows up again in the gospel in a short parable about a fig tree. It was given opportunities of every kind to produce fruit, but it failed to do so. "The Lord is kind and merciful," but he expects us not to take his mercy for granted. With the help of his kindness, he expects us to grow in goodness and holiness.

HOMILY – A young girl brought her boyfriend home to meet her parents. The parents couldn't find many good qualities about him. When the parents had the opportunity to talk to their daughter later, by herself, the girl's mother said: "Dear, he doesn't seem like a very nice person." "Mom," the daughter answered, "if he wasn't nice, why would he be doing 500 hours of community service?"

It's stretching things a bit to say "community service" fits into the theme of today's liturgy, but our readings remind us not to be like the fig tree in Jesus' parable today. We are to produce good works. God didn't create us just to take up space in this world. He wants more from us than that. He wants us to trust him, to love him and to do good for others.

I said in my introduction that the theme for today is "the Lord is kind and merciful." He is kind and merciful in many ways. One of the ways he is kind and merciful is in calling us to repentance and renewal. In the book of Revelation Jesus said: "Whoever is dear to me I reprove and chastise. Be earnest about it, therefore. Repent! Here I stand, knocking at the door. If anyone hears me calling and opens the door, I will enter his house and have supper with him, and he with me." This assumes that we all have room for improvement. God asks that of us and he also gives us the help we need to be better. That is kindness to us. He would not be kind if he didn't stimulate us to keep improving ourselves. The fact that he challenges us to change comes from his love as a caring parent. The parable of the fig tree is a call to live a positive life according to the gospel – doing good by loving God and others.

The conversation Jesus had about tragic events at the beginning of today's gospel was interesting. Sometimes people think when something bad happens to someone it is God's punishment. Jesus said that's not always true. He does not try to explain suffering here, but he is telling us not to be complacent, which we sometimes are. We can't think "well, if nothing bad is happening to me, it must be because I am so good." He tells us we all need to repent, i.e., to work to be better than we are.

This season of Lent keeps reminding us of our need to grow in holiness and goodness. Many people I have talked with do nothing special during Lent. They think they're good enough. Others start off Lent with a great deal of enthusiasm praying more, making sacrifices or doing good work. But as the weeks drag on, they ease up with their good resolutions. We still have four more weeks of Lent. Our readings today are encouraging us to do what we can so we can come to Easter with mind and heart renewed.

Today we have the first of three Scrutinies. Our community prays for those who are preparing to come into the Church at Easter so that they are better able to live the Christian way of life. May we all do a better job of living up to what God wants of us. We must remember, though, at all times, whether God is comforting us, forgiving us, healing us, blessing us, encouraging us or correcting us, "The Lord is kind and merciful."

Fourth Sunday of Lent
March 18, 2007

HOMILY – (Josh 5:9a, 10-12; 2 Cor 5:17-21; Luke 15:1-3, 11-32) We just heard the story of a young boy whose life was misdirected by love of riches and pleasure. After his so called friends abandoned him and he suffered hunger and want for a period of time, he came to his senses and returned to his father. He returned a changed person. Fortunately, he had a loving and forgiving father who accepted him unconditionally. The point of the story is abundantly clear when we consider the relationship between the father and his younger son. As regards the relationship between the father and the older son, Jesus leaves the conclusion open-ended. We have to reflect on what might have happened, whether the older son gave in to his father's pleading to be forgiving or whether he refused. How we end the story will tell us a lot about ourselves.

I want to tell you about another young man whose story is somewhat similar. He was Catholic to start with but admits that he was not a very good one. His father was a government official and this young man enjoyed the comforts of those who were well off. He described himself at sixteen as a scatterbrained youth who had "turned away from God and did not keep his commandments." As his story goes, he was kidnapped and sold as a slave and made to labor on a farm for six years. Like the prodigal son who was without friends and who suffered without adequate food or shelter, this young man came to his senses and he learned obedience through what he suffered. He discovered (and we quote) "God showed me how to have faith in him forever, as one who is never to be doubted." After six years God spoke to him in a way that he heard with his own ears. He would escape and God audibly told him when to leave and what direction to go in order to accomplish his escape. Miraculously God protected him along the way until he arrived back home. Like the prodigal son, he came home a new person. Although his parents wanted to keep him at home with them, his love for God led him to want to serve God as a priest. Even more than serving as a priest, his love for others led him to want to return to the people who captured and enslaved him and teach them about God. And that he did. After overcoming many obstacles, including rejection by the hierarchy, a breach of confidence by a friend to whom he entrusted a confession of his past life, his lack of education and social graces, he returned as a bishop to the people who had enslaved him. Once he arrived he wasn't greeted with open arms. Again, in his own words, he said "daily I expect either murder, or robbery, or enslavement." He writes elsewhere "they seized me with my companions. And on that day they most eagerly desired to kill me; but my time had not yet come. And everything they found with us they plundered, and myself they bound in chains." He feared nothing, for even if he were to be put to death, he felt that would have been the supreme act of love for his God. But God had other intentions than that he should be a martyr. For 30 years he served God and the people who once enslaved him and his work was blessed. He ordained many bishops and priests, established convents, monasteries and schools and in thirty years saw the conversion of almost all of Ireland. And of course you all know I've been talking about St. Patrick, who is one of our patronal saints and whose statue is under the choir loft. His work was so successful that in a short time Ireland was sending out missionaries to revitalize the faith of Europe which had fallen into decline. Irish missionaries have been a blessing to the Church ever since.

For those who are Irish and who honor Patrick, the best way to truly honor him is not by drinking a Guinness. We should respond to his example and his call to holiness. Again quoting Patrick, he asks those who believe in him and love him to "strengthen and confirm your faith...That will be my glory, for a wise son is the glory of his father."

And for those who are not Irish and who think too much is made of St. Patrick on March 17th, I would like you to think of how our faith has been strengthened by the witness of many Irish saints and how our civilization has been preserved by the scholarship of the Irish during the days when mainland Europe was being overrun by barbarians. The great heritage of western civilization, from the Greek and Roman classics to Jewish and Christian works, would have been utterly lost were it not for the holy men and women of unconquered Ireland. These Irish recorded the great works of western civilization in their monasteries and convents (remember all books had to be written by hand). They brought this learning back to Europe after it began to stabilize in the eighth century under Charlemagne. Whether you're Irish or not, we all owe a great debt to the Irish and we pray that our patron, St. Patrick, blesses our parish and our families.

Fifth Sunday of Lent
March 25, 2007

INTRODUCTION – (Isa 43:16-21; Phil 3:8-14; John 8:1-11) Imagine you have been captured by radical Moslems in Iraq, and turned into a slave. Then God sends you a message through a holy person that you will soon be liberated and would be able to come back home. Well, if you can imagine how you would feel, you can imagine how the Jews felt when Isaiah the prophet spoke to them the words in today's first reading. At that time in history, 500 years before Christ, the land we now know as Iraq was known as Babylon. The Jews were their captives and slaves. God tells them their release from the Babylonians would be no less spectacular than their release from slavery in Egypt centuries earlier. Even as the prophet speaks, he tells them the road back to their own land is being made ready. God's statement "see, I am doing something new" leads us into the gospel, where we see Jesus taking a new approach to sinners. He did not come to condemn but to save. His kindness to a woman caught in adultery freed her from both the death sentence and from her sins.

HOMILY – It was God's law. In the book of Leviticus (20,10) and in the book of Deuteronomy (22,22), it states that if a man commits adultery, both the adulterer and the adulteress shall be put to death. The scribes and Pharisees who brought this woman to Jesus acted as if they were interested in observing the law, but they weren't. Otherwise they would have brought both parties to Jesus. The woman wasn't their target, Jesus was. They thought they had him trapped. If he said let her be free, they could accuse him of breaking the Law which he always respected. If he said put her to death, he would be contradicting all he had preached about mercy and forgiveness. In addition, if Jesus said she must be put to death according to the law, he would have been in violation of Roman law, which reserved capital punishment to the Roman governor. And the Romans ruled the Holy Land in the time of Jesus. They thought they had Jesus cornered. No one knows whether he was really writing something or just stalling for time as he moved his finger in the dusty earth. But when they pressed for an answer Jesus said, "Let him who is without sin be the first to cast a stone at her."

I see two moral lessons worth noting in today's gospel.

The first lesson is the most basic of all. Every organization, from the small family unit to the world's largest nations, has to have laws. Without laws, chaos would reign supreme. And there has to be someone to enforce those laws, or they would be meaningless. Jesus observed all God's laws and taught others to do so. He even added a few of his own. But Jesus was able to balance law with mercy. Unfortunately, the notion of mercy is distorted in many people's minds today. They think God is so forgiving that it matters little as to whether they do what God wants or not. Notice Jesus told the lady, "Go, and do not sin again." In the minds of many people, God is an overly permissive parent but God is not. God is a good parent who cares and who loves us and who wants us to be good for our own well being and happiness. That is the first lesson in our gospel: God is merciful, but his mercy is meant to help us lead holier lives. It's not meant to be an excuse to follow the rules he gave us if we like them and ignore the ones we don't.

The second point in today's gospel is this: It relates to judging others. Some people have a responsibility to judge the behavior of others: parents, teachers, doctors, safety personnel like the police, managers, or anyone with authority. We judge the people we vote into office to govern us. That's the beauty of a democracy. We judge people whose behavior affects us in a negative way (like someone driving like an idiot on the expressway). When we make those kinds of judgments that's fair enough, but people don't need our anger, they need our prayers and a patrolman to convince them they can't drive like idiots. But sometimes we get carried away in our tendency to judge others. Especially we tend to consider ourselves better than others because they're not as smart, or as well off, or the same nationality as we are. So we pick up stones to throw at them, stones that frequently are not real stone, but verbal ones: destructive and negative words that tear down. Maybe they're words that we hurl at the offending party. Maybe they're words we pass on to others to hurt the other's reputation. Those destructive words (often called gossip) go around faster than a virus. We need to keep recalling Jesus' words: "Let him who is without sin be the first one to cast a stone at her."

If we consider ourselves as followers of Christ, we have the responsibility to live according to the moral lessons Christ taught us. But let us end with a word of comfort: when we get down on ourselves over our weakness and sins we must remember the Lord is always kind and merciful to those who turn to him for forgiveness.

Passion/Palm Sunday
April 1, 2007

HOMILY – (Isa 50:4-7; Phil 2:6-11; Luke 22:14 – 23:56) Every year on Good Friday we hear the gospel account of Jesus' passion according to John. And every year on Palm Sunday we hear the gospel account of the passion according to one of the other three evangelists. This year we hear from Luke.

I would like to point out three details of Luke's gospel that are unique to him. First of all Luke stresses Jesus' innocence. The Roman governor was the only person in Judea at the time of Jesus who could legally condemn anyone to death. That governor, Pontius Pilate, a man who was noted for his cruelty and who was eventually removed from office by Rome because of his cruelty, declared Jesus innocent in all four gospels. But unlike the other gospels, St. Luke tells us Pilate declared Jesus' innocence, not once or twice, but three separate times. Also, it's only Luke who tells us about the incident with Herod. Most likely to get himself off the hook and avoid condemning an innocent man, Pilate sent Jesus to Herod when he heard Jesus was from the district of Galilee. Herod just happened to be in Jerusalem for the feast of Passover. Although Herod was hoping Jesus would work some miracle, he ended up treating Jesus with contempt when Jesus didn't respond to him. Luke tells us Herod, too, found no charge against him and he sent him back to Pilate. It's only Luke who tells us about the criminal who was crucified with Jesus who declared: "we have been condemned justly... but this man has done nothing wrong." Mark tells us of the centurion who exclaimed when Jesus died: "Truly this man was the Son of God." Luke has the centurion declare, "This man was innocent beyond doubt." The innocent Jesus suffered mockery, violent abuse, injustice, and rejection by his own people. If we were there, would we have been among those who honored him with palms and Hosannas. Or would we have been among those calling for his execution. Or would we simply have been, as many are in our world today, indifferent to it all.

The second characteristic of Jesus that St. Luke emphasizes is his forgiving nature. We see it in all the gospels, but Luke's gospel is especially the gospel of divine mercy. Even as Jesus was on his way to a most cruel and unfair death, he continued to heal and to forgive. All three gospels tell us that at the time of Jesus' arrest, one of his disciples cut off the ear of the high priest's servant. Only St. Luke tells us that Jesus healed the ear. Only St. Luke tells us about the hostility between Pilate and Herod and how, somehow, as a result of Pilate sending Jesus to Herod, they overcame their hatred for each other that day. St. Luke tells us how Jesus forgave those who put him to death: "Father, forgive them, they know not what they do." He even gave forgiveness and promised paradise to the criminal who, with faith, asked Jesus to remember him when he entered his kingdom. Although we are unable to claim to be innocent as Jesus was, we can still follow his example of offering healing and forgiveness rather than hatred and vengeance.

One last detail we probably missed is that Luke does not tell us about the crowning with thorns. He tells us Jesus was mocked and ridiculed, but chooses not to go into the details. Perhaps he felt he had too much more he had to say.

All through my life, meditating on the sufferings of Jesus has given me strength during difficult times. We all have problems in life of one sort or another. Christ's sufferings can give you strength and hope too.

Holy Thursday
April 9, 2009

HOMILY – Fran told me two weeks ago this is the time of the year when people hang up on her when she calls. That's because for years Fran has been so kind as to recruit people for the foot washing. A lot of people avoid talking to her as we get closer to Holy Thursday. People react like Peter: "Fr. Joe will never wash my feet." Well, I'll admit it is humbling to have your pastor kneel in front of you and wash your feet. For me, though, it's not very humbling at all. I think it's very special. But in Jesus' day it was a different story. It was a dirty job. People in those days didn't wear shoes and socks. They wore something more like sandals, and most people walked when they went anywhere. They walked the same dusty, dirty roads that herds of animals walked on. So you can imagine people's feet were dirty and smelly. Having their feet washed when they went to someone's house for dinner would have been refreshing. But the master of the house didn't do the foot washing. Slaves or servants did that job and where there were no slaves or servants, the children or the wife did it. I suppose if I wanted to be really humble, I would go wash the feet of several homeless people and have no audience or pretty singing while I was doing it. But we do it tonight to dramatize what Jesus did.

One of our candidates for foot washing remarked, "I don't know what to think about this." Well, Jesus did a lot of teaching and a lot of healing and helping people. But this last night with his apostles before his death, he wanted to really do something off the wall that would stick with them and symbolize what he was all about. So he told them how to think about what he had done. He said: "I have given you a model to follow, so that as I have done for you, you should also do." He had previously told us, "Whoever wishes to be great among you must be your servant, and whoever wishes to be first among you must be your slave." He gave us an example of the great commandment of love; that we should love one another as he has loved us.

But there was an interesting interchange between Jesus and Peter. When Jesus came to Peter, Peter basically asked, "why are you going to wash my feet?" Jesus said, "you don't understand now why I'm doing it, you will understand later." Peter protested, "you will never wash my feet." Jesus said (and I like this translation better), "If I do not wash you, you won't belong to me." That is as strong a statement as Jesus could have made. I asked myself why Jesus was so definite and why was it was so important that everyone have their feet washed, even Peter? Thinking of what Jesus was doing as a demonstration of service, it struck me that we all need to allow ourselves to let Jesus serve us. In what ways does he serve us? He serves us through his sacrificial death on the cross and his resurrection. In his words, he came to seek out and to save the one who is lost; and that's all of us. It's only when we know we need to be saved that we will really know Jesus for that's what the name "Jesus" means: God saves. How do we make this connection with his saving love? Two ways: prayer and the sacraments. In those two ways Jesus can serve us and save us.

Especially in the Eucharist does Jesus come to us to bring us the love and life he wants to share with us. He makes himself vulnerable to us. We can receive him with love, we can receive him with indifference, we can receive him with distraction, we can be too busy to bother coming to receive him at all. But for those who open the door of their heart to him, he is there to share a meal with us as friends. (Rev. 3, 20) What greater gift can he give us than himself. "My flesh is real food and my blood real drink," he tells us in John's sixth chapter on the Eucharist.

Tonight we recall Jesus' last supper with his disciples. He came to serve them and he did serve them as their teacher and Lord, but now he was about to serve them (and all of us) by his death on a cross. He demonstrated to us how we are to serve one another and gave us a command to do so. And at the Last Supper he gave us a way to remember what he has done for us and how he continues to bring us into union with his saving work, the Eucharist. "Do this in memory of me" we hear him say twice in tonight's second reading, the oldest recorded account of the institution of the Eucharist.

We may not understand it all, we may not understand why Jesus had to die to save us, we may not understand how a small host and a sip of wine can bring Jesus to us, we may not even understand why God would love us so much as to send his Son to save us, but as Jesus said to Peter: "you will understand later." Amen.

Good Friday
April 6, 2007

HOMILY – (Isa 52:13-53:12; Heb 4:14-16; 5:7-9; John 18:1-19:42) Jesus was a good man who came to preach, to heal, to teach us how to love God and to love others. He chose to remain faithful to his mission no matter what it cost him. And indeed it cost him. Crucifixion was one of the most horrible forms of torture ever devised by human beings throughout recorded history.

Other than reminding us of our own potential for cruelty or reminding us of Christ's faithfulness to his mission, we have to look at Jesus' death from the perspective of whom it was who suffered.

He wasn't just some great person out of history. He wasn't just some holy man, or a good teacher, or a powerful healer, or an altruistic fellow. He was the Son of God. He was God who took on our human flesh, who got tired and hungry and thirsty, who walked the dusty roads everyone else walked, but whose love was greater than any one of us can begin to imagine. He was God who, in love, kept doing good for the people he loved – even in the face of betrayal, denial, abandonment, beating, ridicule, false accusations, and crucifixion.

Lots of people in the course of history have given their lives for others. Lots of soldiers have made the supreme sacrifice in defending their loved ones in battle. But Jesus' death was different than that. His death opens up a new world for us, a new vision of God. His death gives a new meaning to human suffering and death, showing us that God can take our crosses and defeats and turn them into the possibility of new life for us.

Of course, all the gospels stress Jesus' divinity, but John's gospel pictures it so much more clearly. Jesus is in control of the whole event. Jesus knew Judas was turning him in; he knew the Jewish leaders would come to get him. He didn't try to run away. John doesn't deny the terrible agony in the garden; he just doesn't mention it. When Jesus identifies himself, the forces of Satan fall back in the presence of the great I AM. (The Greek says "I am.") He tells the soldiers, if I am the one you want, let these men go. He discourages Peter's efforts to beat off his enemies with a sword. Jesus is in charge of the situation.

Before Pilate, Jesus answers the governor with dignity and honesty. Soon we see Pilate squirming in an effort to get out of making the decision of condemning a man he knew was innocent. He tried to stir up the sympathy of the people by humiliating Jesus and having him scourged, but he finally caved in to the crowd. The crime Jesus was charged with announced to the world in Hebrew, Greek, and Latin – that Jesus was king of the Jews.

Jesus carried his own cross. John doesn't tell us about Simon of Cyrene who was called into service to help him carry it. On the cross, Jesus doesn't cry out "My God, my God ..." Instead he makes provisions for his mother. He is even in charge of the moment of death when he announced "It is finished."

We're not going to figure out this mystery of divine love today, or even this year, or in a lifetime. (Inserted the story of the Zen master.) Some saints may have gained a depth of understanding which sent them into ecstasy, but most of us just keep trying – but that's all right.

That's why we commemorate Jesus' death and resurrection every day and every week. That's why Jesus said "do this in memory of me," because both Our Lord and the Church knows we have to keep remembering it, thinking about it, understanding it differently as we grow and mature and encounter new life challenges.

Jesus' death is one of the central mysteries of our faith, the key act of God that offers us eternal life. But it is not his death alone that saves us; it is his resurrection too. (Christ died for our sins . . .) So again we recall what Jesus did for us, trying to understand the whole mystery a little better. We are solemn and somber, yet we know we are celebrating too, (it is after all "Good Friday). We celebrate the event by which we are saved, and celebrate an infinite love which we do not yet understand but in which the cross helps us to believe.

Easter
April 8, 2007

HOMILY – (Acts 10:34a, 37-43; Col 3:1-4; John 20:1-9) A week before Easter, a Sunday school teacher was teaching her class of little children about Jesus' seven last words on the cross. Finally she asked "What was the last thing Jesus said before he died?" A little boy raised his hand and answered: "He said: 'I'll be back.'"

A father was trying to get his two sons to eat a healthy lunch after they had stuffed themselves with Easter candy. After several failed attempts his wife said to him "It's Easter Sunday. What do you expect, a miracle?"

What would it be like if there were no spring, if winter just stayed on and on (as it seems to be doing)? It would embarrass all the global warming people but worse than that. All life would eventually die. Our world would become a frozen lifeless body floating in space. Our spiritual life without Easter would be like our world without spring, for the death and resurrection of Jesus is the source of our life in God. There is no day of the entire year that can compare with Easter. Not even Christmas would be celebrated if there were no Easter for without Easter it is unlikely we would ever have even heard of Jesus. If he had not risen, his small group of followers would have drifted apart. It was only the resurrection, along with the sending of the Spirit, that gave his followers the courage and the purpose to go on talking about him.

It always seems at this time of the year the media comes out with some kind of book or movie or TV program that tries to make people question the reality of the death or the resurrection of Jesus. They have to find something controversial no matter how obscure it may be. We cannot prove the resurrection scientifically. It is a matter of faith. As a doctrine of faith, it is not something that someone just dreamed up one day. There is a solid foundation for the faith that we have in the resurrection of Jesus. What is that foundation? We have an empty tomb, a tomb that has been venerated by believers from the earliest days of the Church. It still is, even after it had been buried for 200 years under a temple built to honor the Greek goddess, Aphrodite. Most likely the shroud of Turin, the cloth in which Jesus' body was laid to rest, provides a basis for the resurrection of Jesus. The strongest evidence, in my mind, is the witness of Jesus' apostles to the resurrection. They were not a gullible bunch who were expecting the resurrection or were looking for it to happen. We have the story of the doubting Thomas, which we will hear next week, that illustrates it. It was the appearances of Jesus to the Apostles that convinced them Jesus truly had risen. The resurrection of Jesus wasn't something they believed in as we have to believe in it – it was something they had seen for themselves. They witnessed to it. In Greek the word for witness is martyria (μαρτυρία). This indicates what happened to the apostles for standing by their story that Jesus had risen and had appeared to them many times. They had nothing to gain in a worldly way by witnessing to Jesus' resurrection. They only brought suffering and eventual martyrdom upon themselves by doing so. Like their master, they were faithful to what they proclaimed no matter what.

Our faith is founded on that witness, a witness that goes back to the beginning. In our faith we find hope, hope that there is a way out of any darkness, hope that God can take any disaster, any tragedy and make something good come out of it. If we have sinned, if we have suffered something terrible, it is not beyond redemption. God can transform it. The empty tomb gives us hope, hope that death is not the end of our existence, hope that death is not the end of life for those we love. Easter is the answer to all the tears that we shed at the graves of our loved ones because it tells us God has better things planned for us.

If we truly believe in Easter, then we have to live a new life. Paul tells us we are to be intent on things above rather than on things of earth. If Christ's resurrection does not begin to transform us now, when will it begin to do so? We can't wait for death to catch up with us. Sharing Christ's risen life must begin now through the grace he gives us in the sacraments.

Today God reveals not only the resurrection of his Son. God also shows us his plans for all who are his sons and daughters. May the hope of the new life of Christ fill your hearts today with Alleluia.

2nd Sunday of Easter
April 15, 2007

INTRODUCTION – (Acts 5:12-16; Rev 1:9-11a, 12-13, 17-19; John 20:19-31) The four gospels tell us about Jesus' life, death, and resurrection. Essentially, the rest of the new testament tells us about Jesus after his resurrection and ascension, how he continued his work through his followers and through the Church.

In the first reading from the Acts of the Apostles we see the power of Jesus at work through the signs and wonders that the apostles worked. Our second reading is from the book of Revelation. Most probably this book was written sometime between 81 and 96 AD, during the reign of the Emperor Domitian. It was a time of persecution for the Church. John tells us in today's passage he was in exile on a little island called Patmos as punishment for preaching about Jesus. The Lord appeared to him there and revealed to him that Jesus would not abandon those who were faithful to him. Those suffering for their faith in Jesus would be victorious in the end.

HOMILY – Woody Allen is quoted as saying: "if only God would give me some clear sign! Like making a large deposit in my name at a Swiss bank." Our gospel today invites us to reflect on the meaning of faith. If God gave us all clear signs, we wouldn't need faith. Faith essentially means trusting someone when we have no clear signs. Faith is not the same as putting our trust in anyone and everyone. That's just being naive and gullible. At the same time, if we are afraid to trust anyone we will live in our own little world of fear and paranoia. It's a difficult balance to keep knowing who we can and who we cannot trust.

One person we can trust is Jesus. In our second reading, Jesus appeared to John and told him "Do not be afraid." Fear is the opposite of trust. When he tells us do not be afraid, he is telling us to trust him. He is the master over life and death, for as he said, "I hold the keys to death."

Another way of saying all this is Jesus' greeting to his apostles on Easter Sunday night: "Peace be with you." A person full of fear and anxiety and worry does not know peace. Before we know peace we have to know who we can trust and know that our trust is secure.

Our trust is secure in Jesus but we all wish the Lord would give us a little more proof, as he did to Thomas. Three times John's gospel tells us Thomas was called the twin. Why do you think John made such a point of the fact that he was a twin? Perhaps in a symbolic way we are his twin, wanting proof like he did. Thomas wouldn't believe in the resurrection of Jesus, even with the other ten apostles and some of the women telling him it happened. But I still have to give Thomas credit. He could have walked away and said "you're all crazy. I'm getting out of here." He stayed with them through what must have been a very difficult week for him. I think there's a lesson here. When we have doubts and questions about our faith, we need to stay with it and not walk away. If Thomas had walked away, he would never have seen the Lord. The gospel is telling us, if we stay with it, the Lord will reveal himself to us. We will see him and know him, maybe not with our eyes, but with our mind and heart.

A lot of times we hear people say: "seeing is believing." What they are really saying is they don't believe one word we're saying, because believing is accepting something without seeing it. Seeing is not believing, but with God the opposite is true according to the gospel. Believing will lead to seeing. But we have to believe first. We have to trust in what we hear (the words of Jesus) rather than in what we see (for the Lord tells us about things that are unseen). And we trust in what we hear because we choose to trust Jesus.

One of the greatest challenges to our faith today is the Eucharist. Jesus told us: "This is my body... this is my blood." Because we can't put the Eucharist under a microscope or examine it in some other way and see Jesus there, many people say "This is just a symbol. This is just a reminder of what Jesus did at the Last Supper. It's not really his body and blood." The gospels and the earliest tradition of the Church tell us the Eucharist is exactly what Jesus said it is. I think the decline in Mass attendance can be explained in large part by the fact that people have lost faith in the Eucharist. Jesus' words to Thomas apply to us as we gather together today in faith: "Blessed (a word with also means 'fortunate' or 'happy') are those who have not seen and have believed."

3rd Sunday of Easter
April 22, 2007

INTRODUCTION – (Acts 5:27-32, 40b-41; Rev 5:11-14; John 21:1-19) The glory of the risen Lord is reflected in today's readings. Before commenting on our first reading, it is worth pointing out the symbolism in the second reading from the book of Revelation. The setting for the scene is in heaven. The focus is on Christ, symbolized as a sacrificial lamb who reigns gloriously with God the Father. It is worth commenting on this symbol because it is the symbol on the front of our altar. The lamb is standing on a book in which was written the revelation of what was to come. Only Jesus was worthy to break open the seven seals that kept the book from being opened. In today's reading the liturgy of praise being offered to Jesus recognizes his divinity and his equality with the Father.

And now about today's first reading. Immediately prior to today's reading the apostles Peter and John, in the name of Jesus, healed a crippled man in the Temple. This gave Peter the opportunity to preach about the risen Lord and it led to the arrest of Peter and John. They were warned not to preach about Jesus again and were released. They continued to preach and, that time after their arrest, were thrown into jail. In the middle of the night an angel released them from jail and they went right back to preaching about Jesus. It wasn't long before they were arrested for the third time and this is where our first reading comes in. Today's passage leaves out a few verses which I think are very important. Those verses tell us that as a punishment for disobeying the various warning of the court not to preach about Jesus, the apostles were scourged, then they were set free. What is remarkable is they were joyful about it; they felt honored to have suffered for the name of the Lord.

HOMILY – John tells us the apostles had been fishing all night and they caught nothing. As the sun was coming up Jesus appeared to them. He not only gave them all the fish they could handle but was busy getting breakfast ready for them. On the surface John is simply describing the scene for us in this lovely story of one of Jesus' appearances after the resurrection. But, as often happens in John's gospel, there is a deeper meaning in what he is telling us. In this passage about night and dawn, darkness and light, John is doing more than simply telling us the time of day. Let me explain what I mean.

John's gospel begins with the words "In the beginning..." What's so important about these words? These are the very words that begin the whole bible, the first words from the book of Genesis. What does that have to do with light and darkness? When God began to create the world, the first thing he created was light. So after John begins his gospel by telling us "in the beginning was the word and the word was with God and the word was God," he goes on to tell us: "He created everything there is. Nothing exists that he didn't make. Life itself was in him and this life was light for all people." John's theme continues that not everyone accepted the light, but the light was unable to be put out.

The image of light and darkness continues to weave it's way through John. In chapter three we hear about a Pharisee named Nicodemus who was curious to learn more from Jesus, and he came to Jesus at night. It was a practical thing to do considering the hostility against Jesus, but a symbolic detail for John as well. Nicodemus was seeking the light and until he was enlightened by Jesus, he was in the dark.

Again, in the ninth chapter of John we hear about Jesus healing a man born blind. The whole chapter contrasts the blindness of the Pharisees, people who had sight but whose minds and hearts were closed to the light, with the insights of the blind man, the one who lived in darkness all his life until he met Jesus. In this chapter Jesus says clearly, "I am the light of the world."

When we get to the Last Supper in John's gospel, we find a little sentence that might not seem important all by itself but, knowing John's symbolism, it has a depth of meaning. Judas was about to betray Jesus. As he left the supper room John tells us "it was night." For Judas it was night as he walked off into the darkness!

So when we hear today's gospel, we are told the apostles were fishing all night. What did they accomplish? Without Jesus they accomplished nothing. With the dawn the Lord showed up, the one who is the Light of the world, and everything changes. Are there times when we feel like we're working hard and going nowhere? Perhaps reflecting on St. John's themes of light and darkness in today's gospel will remind us of Jesus' words from the Last Supper: "without me you can do nothing?"

4th Sunday of Easter
April 29, 2007

INTRODUCTION – (Acts 13:14, 43-52; Rev 7:9, 14b-17; John 10:27-30); The first reading describes the Church in the early days of the apostles. We hear about two of them: Saints Paul and Barnabas. It was during Paul's first missionary journey. He and Barnabas were in the area we today know as Turkey. There were communities of Jews scattered throughout the Roman Empire. Some of those communities even had synagogues if they were large or prosperous enough. Paul visited one of those synagogues and, since he was a Pharisee, he was invited to preach to the people. His message was so powerful he was asked to return and preach on the following Sabbath. This is where our first reading comes in. He packed the house, but many of the Jews responded negatively to his message. This didn't discourage the apostles. They went on to preach to the pagan Gentiles. Notice the apostles were filled with joy in spite of rejection. They knew they were doing Christ's work and that the Spirit was leading them.

Today's second reading is a vision of the Church in heaven from the book of Revelation. This vision of heaven was meant to be an encouragement to early Christians to keep following our Lord in spite of a bitter persecution against them. Here Christ is pictured as a Lamb. The image of the lamb symbolized Jesus' sacrifice for us since lambs were so frequently offered in sacrifice in the Old Testament. We use this image still when we refer to Jesus as the Lamb of God. At the end of the reading a second image of Christ is introduced: the lamb of God as our shepherd. But, as he tells us in the gospel, that is true only to the extent that we hear his voice.

HOMILY – If we lived in Israel at the time of Jesus, we would instantly relate to what Jesus told us today in the gospel. Sheep were the people's main source of meat, milk and cheese. They provided wool for clothing. And they were regularly used as sacrifice in their liturgy.

If I were to try to think of something in our culture today that would be similar to the relationship of a shepherd to his sheep, the best comparison I can come up with is a mother who needs to be home to care for several toddlers. Just as toddlers depend on their mother's care, and their mother is always busy, sheep depend on the care of their shepherd and the shepherd, who has dozens of sheep, is kept busy 24 hours a day, seven days a week.

Today's gospel makes reference to an activity that shepherds had to go through daily. When night came, a number of shepherds would come together with their sheep and put them in a pen. Then they would sleep while one shepherd would stay awake watching out for thieves or predatory animals. In the morning, each shepherd would call out for his own sheep to follow him to pasture. The sheep knew the voice of their own shepherd and would follow only their own shepherd's voice when they were called. They would ignore all the other shepherds who were calling for their sheep. The gospel reflects this when Jesus said, "My sheep hear my voice; I know them and they follow me."

Some people are offended to hear themselves compared to sheep. Perhaps that's because they don't realize they need God's constant care at all times and not just when they have problems.

We live in a society where everyone is trying to get our attention. You can't turn on the radio or TV without someone trying to sell you something. Even to go for a drive, you have billboards trying to catch your eye. Companies spend significant amounts of money to buy just 30 seconds of advertising time in order to get their message across. Sometimes, like sheep, we just follow the latest message we hear or sometimes we hear so many messages and, like sheep, we just follow the crowd. Jesus says, "My sheep hear my voice." If we want to belong to him, we do have to hear his voice. Though in today's world it takes a conscious effort to do so. We have to take time to shut out all kinds of other noises so we can listen to him. If we don't make the effort, we can easily lose touch with our shepherd. This is one reason (among many) to take time to pray and to come to church every Sunday. We need to keep in touch.

Our Lord does not want to lose any one of us. His desire is for us to be with him forever, in heaven, where there will be no more sadness or pain, where as our second reading tells us, he will wipe every tear from our eyes. One of the ways he leads us is through the Eucharist we are celebrating. He is with us as we gather in his name, he speaks to us in Scriptures, he feeds us with his own body and blood. Sheep may not be smart, but they are smart enough to know they need their shepherd and to recognize his voice. Let us pray we are always smart enough to know we need our Shepherd and to listen for his voice.

5th Sunday of Easter
May 6, 2007

INTRODUCTION – (Acts 14:21-27; Rev 21:1-5a; John 13:31-33a, 34-35) Last Sunday we heard a little bit about Paul's first missionary journey. He won many converts and at the same time ran into many obstacles and much opposition. Today's first reading is still part of Paul's first journey as he makes his return trip back to the Church in Antioch in Syria. He is revisiting cities where he had already preached. The names of the cities are all foreign to us, and today's reading could confuse us in that there were two cities named Antioch. The first Antioch mentioned here was one of the cities which he and Barnabas had visited in what is today Turkey. It was one of the cities that rejected Paul. The second Antioch, in Syria, was one of the four largest cities in the Roman Empire. This Christian community was the one who initially sent Paul and Barnabas out to evangelize. Paul was returning to report how things went. He acknowledged that at times it wasn't easy.

HOMILY – We're obsessed with what's new. We often greet one another that way. The media invests heavily in keeping up-to-date with the news. Businesses work hard to create new products, new ideas, and new ways of doing things. Research and industry are giving us new ways to save lives as well as new ways to destroy them. We look for new ways to have fun and to find happiness. Thus all of us should be able to relate to God's words in today's reading from the Book of Revelation: "Behold, I make all things new." It is not just a new product or new idea God is bringing about. It will be so all encompassing, so radically new and wonderful, that the visionary tells us it will be a new heavens and a new earth.

The book of Revelations can only provide hints of what this new heavens and new earth will be like. For starters, there will be no more suffering or sickness or pain. Death will be done away with. We shall never have to say good-bye to those we love. God will wipe away every tear from our eyes. We will be totally transformed. We will all love each other. There will be no more wars or killing or hunger or poverty or prejudice or terrorism. Would you vote for that or do you think it might be too boring?

Well, it is up to us to vote for because we will have a hand in making this new world come about. We want God to come along and wave a magic wand to make it happen. But it won't happen that way. We have to be involved in the process. It's just as if someone invented a medicine that would eliminate cancer; it wouldn't help a person with cancer unless they took the medicine. In a similar way God can't create a new world if we don't help him, if we desire to hold on to the cancer of hatred and jealousy and lustful pleasures and unforgiveness and self-righteous pride.

The new world will come about by living the gospel, by sharing in Christ's risen life, by loving one another as he has loved us – as he tells us in today's gospel. This is not always easy. St. Paul warns us it will not always be easy as he tells us in today's first reading: "It is necessary for us to undergo many hardships to enter the kingdom of God."

The trials Paul was talking about in this passage were the trials of persecution. Compared to what the early Christians had to go through to keep the faith, we have it really easy. We don't have to face the sword or crucifixion or lions in the coliseum. For most of us today, the trials we have to face are basically the trials of trying to be faithful to prayer, to the sacraments, and to God's commandments.

When we think of this new world that God is creating, we usually think of heaven. That can give us a lot of hope and encouragement right now. Certainly we will experience all that God promised us and more in heaven, but God is making all things new right now. We can choose to be part of that process or we can just get in the way.

In the Eucharist we are celebrating today, he is inviting us to share with him in this process of creation. Through the Eucharist he touches our lives with his new life and love as we come together in prayer and faith. He speaks to us in the Scriptures, he prays with us as our high priest, he feeds us with his own body and blood to strengthen us and nourish us. [Today we have with us three children from our parish who are going to receive the Eucharist for the first time. The Eucharist is spiritual food which nourishes the risen life of Christ in us and which helps his life in us to grow and deepen. Just as we need to eat every day to stay strong and healthy, so the Eucharist is creating newness of life in us. May you grow each week from this holy food which you will receive for the first time today.] It is only in Christ and by living his life now that a new world will come to be, both now and in eternity. Without him we are like a lamp that is not plugged in. We cannot shine. With him we have the power to love like him, the power to live a new life, and the power to create a new world. Amen.

6th Sunday of Easter
May 13, 2007

INTRODUCTION – (Acts 15:1-2, 22-29; Rev 21:10-14, 22-23; John 14:23-29) The first followers of Christ were all Jewish. They continued to follow their Jewish customs and traditions. When Gentiles also started to believe in Jesus, there was conflict. Many Jewish converts insisted that Gentiles had to adopt Jewish ways if they wanted to consider themselves followers of Jesus. The problem arose especially in Antioch, in Syria, one of the four largest cities in the Roman Empire and racially quite diverse. The setting for our first reading is in Antioch.

HOMILY – I have to tell you a couple of cute stories about moms. Mary was on the way to visit her mother. She had her teenage daughter in the car with her and on the way she commented to her daughter, "Dear, your skirt is a little short isn't it? Her daughter gave her that look: "Oh Mom!" When she arrived at her mother's house, she came in and her mother remarked to Mary: "Dear, your neckline is a little low, isn't it?" Once a mom, always a mom.!

A working mom was out of town at a business conference and, not having a cell phone handy, she called home collect. Her young son answered the phone and the operator spoke: "I have a Betty Smith on the phone. Will you accept charges?" He dropped the phone and ran into the kitchen to where his father was and screamed out: "They got mom and they want money." No amount of money can measure the value of a good mom."

Today is Mother's Day and I wish a blessed day to all our mothers and grandmothers and substitute mothers. Friday we honored Mary, Jesus' mother and ours, and that's why the statue of Mary is here today. It's an appropriate day to remember Mary our mother.

The events described in our first reading occurred about the year 50 A.D. If you think this issue is irrelevant, consider what the Church might be like today if the apostles decided that all converts to Christ had to follow Jewish ritual, feast days and dietary laws. The nations, by and large, might have rejected Christianity and we would still be worshipping pagan gods. Perhaps we would be avoiding pork and insisting our baby boys be circumcised. We might be learning to read the Old Testament in Hebrew and keeping other Jewish traditions and customs. Notice how the Apostles introduced their decision: "It is the decision of the Holy Spirit, and ours too..." This has always been the belief of the Church whenever the bishops gather in council together with the Holy Father. It is an important concept especially today when so many people think they do not need any authority in the Church telling them what's right or wrong. Christ gave his Spirit to his Church to lead us to holiness.

I want to talk especially about heaven today. Today's second reading is an excerpt from the book of Revelation where heaven is described. At the time this book was written, the early Christians were suffering under a bitter persecution. It was written to give them encouragement and hope. The description of heaven (a.k.a. the heavenly Jerusalem) is awesome. If you get out your bibles, you will get much more of a description of the heavenly Jerusalem than our brief reading today gives us. In those days a city was surrounded by a wall to protect the inhabitants of the city from wild animals and enemies. The wall of the heavenly Jerusalem was high, 1500 miles high, and broad, 1500 miles in four directions, forming a perfect cube. The wall was over 200 feet thick. Quite a bit of protection there. The foundation stones for the wall were various gems on which the names of the twelve apostles were written, showing the city is founded on the apostles. We've all heard jokes about what happens at heaven's gate, but notice there are twelve gates. The gates of the city, open in all four directions, indicate that God's kingdom is open to all people. The gates are each made of a single pearl (thus the term: the pearly gates). The gates have inscribed on them the names of the twelve tribes of Israel indicating the Old Testament roots of our faith. The dimensions of the city would be about half the size of the United States! That's some city. The size symbolizes the multitude of people that will fill God's kingdom. The city was pure gold, clear as glass, and the streets of the city were pure gold. I've told this joke before about the guy who made a deal with God. He asked God to allow him to take one thing with him when he died. God said okay, so he chose to take all his gold with him. When he died and arrived in heaven, lugging his satchel of gold, St. Peter asked him what he was going to do with that big bag of pavement. Of course all this is symbolic. It's the Bible's best attempt to describe the glory of heaven. The city is described as coming down out of heaven from God. It other words, God is its source, and it is not here yet, but it's on its way for those who are faithful.

The city is without a temple for we will experience God directly. No temple will be needed. It needs no light for it's source of light is God, who is the fullness of light. The gates are never shut during the day, and since it is always day, the gates are never shut. That means God holds out his invitation to all who will answer. But it also tells us not everyone answers. No one evil shall enter the city. They have shut themselves out.

In our common way of thinking of heaven, we picture God deciding on who comes in or who doesn't. This is a simple way of expressing a more abstract truth. A life of holiness will lead to happiness and a life of wrongdoing will lead to unhappiness. In reality, however, it is not God who decides who gets in and who doesn't. That decision is made by each of us. That is what today's gospel teaches us. Something has to happen in a person's life before they can "get into" heaven. Heaven has to "get into" them. Jesus tells us "whoever loves me will keep my word, and my Father will love him, and we will come to him and make our dwelling with him." Having God in us, living in us, animating us with his grace, loving us with his infinite love, uniting us with one another through his Spirit is what will constitute the glory of heaven. Instead of worrying whether we will be "in" or "out," our focus should be on whether and to what extent we are letting God "in," having time for him, serving him or whether we're too busy to pray or to give him our time or our service.

Feast of the Ascension of the Lord
May 20, 2007

INTRODUCTION – (Acts 1:1-11; Heb 9:24-28; 10:19-23; Luke 24:46-53) St. Luke gave us two books in the New Testament: The Acts of the Apostles and, of course, his gospel. We hear from both of them today. The gospel ends with the ascension and the Acts of the Apostles begins with the ascension. You'll notice when you hear the first reading from the Acts, he refers to his gospel as his "first book." It is interesting how he treats the ascension in each of these two books. In the Acts he said Jesus ascended 40 days after Easter, but in his gospel he describes how Jesus appeared to his apostles Easter Sunday night, spoke with them, ate with them and then, that night, he led them out to Bethany where he ascended into heaven. It seems as if Jesus' physical departure from the apostles and his return to the Father was not a one-time dramatic event. It was more like a process. One way of thinking of the 40-day period is that after the resurrection Jesus appeared rather frequently to the apostles. Luke's description of the ascension 40 days after Easter seems to mark the end of those frequent appearances. After that Jesus would be present to his followers through the Holy Spirit, the sacraments, and the Church. Luke's second book, the Acts of the Apostles, tells us of the ways Christ continues to be with us through the Holy Spirit, the sacraments, and the Church.

HOMILY – St. Luke's gospel begins in the temple of Jerusalem with the angel Gabriel announcing to the old priest Zechariah that he and his elderly wife, Elizabeth, would have a baby boy. The angel Gabriel said to him

"Do not be afraid, Zechariah, for your prayer is heard, and your wife Elizabeth will bear you a son, and you shall call his name John. And you will have joy and gladness, and many will rejoice at his birth." The joy at the birth of John the Baptist was only the beginning of many moments of joy recorded by St. Luke. A few months after Gabriel appeared to Zechariah, he appeared to Mary and asked her to be the mother of our Savior. She said "yes," as we know, and then she immediately sought out her cousin Elizabeth with her good news. Mary expressed herself in the beautiful canticle, the Magnificat: "My soul proclaims the greatness of the Lord, and my spirit rejoices in God my Savior." When Jesus was born, it was the shepherds who heard the message of joy. The angel said to them: "Do not be afraid; for behold, I bring you good news of great joy that will be for all the people." I could bore you with a number of Luke's other references to joy, but I'll just fast forward to the ending of his gospel as we just heard.

St. Luke's gospel began in the Temple of Jerusalem and that's where it ends. It also ends with a note of joy, the same sentiment with which it began. After the ascension of Jesus, Luke tells us as Jesus "parted from them and was taken up to heaven, they did him homage and then returned to Jerusalem with great joy, and they were continually in the temple praising God."

Wouldn't you think the apostles would have been depressed when Jesus left them? If they were thinking only on an earthly level, of course they would have been. For it is natural to grieve when we lose someone who is important to us. But instead of grieving they "returned to Jerusalem with great joy." I can think of at least four reasons why they were so joyful. 1) Jesus had assured them they weren't really losing him. He would still be with them. He assured them, as we heard last Sunday, "whoever loves me will keep my word, and my Father will love him, and we will come to him and make our dwelling with him." 2) They were joyful because they were happy for him and they loved him enough not to begrudge his return to the Father. After all he did say: "if you truly loved me you would rejoice to have me go to the Father." 3) They were joyful because they knew there were better things ahead. There was the Spirit which they didn't understand yet, but which they trusted to be something wonderful. Jesus told them: "It is better for you that I go, for if I do not go, the Holy Spirit will not come to you." And 4) they knew one day they would be with the Lord forever. He told them he was going to get a place ready for them: "and, if I go and prepare a place for you, I will come back again and take you to myself, so that where I am you also may be."

They would have had no joy if they thought only of their separation from him. After his resurrection they began to see him in a different way. Luke even tells us they "did him homage," a term reserved for worship of God. Their new way of seeing Jesus gave them new faith and hope and love. They could only rejoice in the faith, hope and love that filled them. Can we too rejoice in the ascension of our Lord?

Vigil of Pentecost
May 26, 2007

HOMILY – (Ezek 37:1-14; Rom 8:22-27; John 7:37-39) If you happen to look for today's readings anywhere, you would be very confused. Between the Vigil Mass this afternoon and today's feast, thirteen different readings are offered for our use. And these thirteen readings hardly touch all the references to the Spirit in the Scriptures. All these optional readings, some for the

Vigil and some for today, tell us this is not an ordinary Sunday. And we have a sequence, a poem about the Spirit, before the Gospel. The only other feast that has a required sequence that I can think of is Easter. Corpus Christi has an optional one. The fact that there are a lot of people in church wearing red also tells us there is something special about today. Special indeed! It's the third most important feast of the entire year. Without the Holy Spirit nothing would have happened. The apostles would have remained a frightened bunch of guys who would have been afraid of their own shadow. They certainly wouldn't have risked their lives to preach about the Risen Christ. Without the Holy Spirit the gospels would not have been written. We would probably still be worshipping plants or animals or inanimate objects as our gods if we were worshiping anything at all.

I came across an interesting illustration that might help us understand the Holy Spirit and thus the place of Pentecost in our lives. The Flemish artist, Rubens, like other artists of his time, had a group of aspiring artists working with him. As he watched them at work, he would sometimes pause for a moment as he looked over their shoulders, then he would take the paint brush from the hands of his pupil and would add the finishing touches. It was those touches which brought the painting to life. After referring to this practice of Rubens, a modern scripture scholar noted that until the day of Pentecost the disciples, our Lord's pupils, (for disciple means learner) had been clumsily trying to be like their Master, "but on that day the Spirit finished the painting."

It is a neat way of summarizing the effects of the first Pentecost. It explains why Pentecost is spoken of as the Church's birthday, the day when the Church truly sprang to life; the day when it was made ready for its mission of taking the Good News to the ends of the earth.

Although the mighty wind, which shook the house where the disciples had gathered, soon grew still; the flames of fire which hovered over their heads, soon disappeared. But the Holy Spirit, whose coming had been announced by wind and fire, came to stay and came to be with the Church until the end of time: to be its very soul, its life principle.

Our first reading today is one of my favorites. At the time of Ezekiel there was no understand of the Trinity nor was there any idea of individual resurrection. Ezekiel here is referring to the nation of Israel that was at that time in Exile in Babylon. They had given up hope of ever returning home or of ever being a nation again. Ezekiel is telling them God would bring them back from exile and raise them up. But here the function of God's Spirit as a life giving Spirit is already apparent.

Paul in the second reading tells us the Spirit has come to us, but the fullness of life the Spirit brings is still in the process of formation within us. And the Spirit is there to help it come to be.

Jesus in today's gospel compares the Spirit to water. Why water? Because water brings life. Without it life cannot exist.

When most people think of the Spirit, they think of the personal gifts the Spirit brings them. Before I studied Scripture in the Seminary, the only time I ever thought of the Spirit was when I had to pass an exam. But that's only one of the functions of the Spirit, the Spirit of truth, a term for the Spirit that Jesus uses. But there are many other gifts the Spirit brings. The Spirit helps us in our prayers, St. Paul tells us. (Rom 8, 26) In the letter to the Galatians St. Paul names a variety of blessings the Spirit brings to each of us: love, joy, peace, patience, kindness, generosity, faithfulness, gentleness and self-control (Gal. 5,22). Wouldn't it be wonderful to have all those qualities? Wouldn't it be wonderful if all the people we associate with, if all people in the world, had all these qualities. The Spirit has a lot of work to do.

But the Spirit is interested in more than blessing each of us personally. The Spirit is also a source of life for the Church. Paul tells us the Spirit gives many special gifts to the faith community so it might be well served. Among these gifts are wisdom, faith, healing, the gift of speaking God's word, the gift of discernment, the gift of helping others, the gift of administration and the gift of being able to council others. (I Cor 12). What gifts has the Spirit given us and how do we use them to serve others. The Spirit helps people do more than pass exams. The Spirit is the "Lord and giver of life" as we profess each week in the Creed. The Spirit is the giver of our spiritual life which will endure forever as well as the giver of life to the Church. There would be no Church without the Spirit.

On this Pentecost, I pray may the Holy Spirit put the finishing touches to our small efforts, to follow Christ faithfully and to bring about a miniature Pentecost in our midst and so renew the face of the earth.

Pentecost
June 4, 2006

HOMILY – (Acts 2, 1-11; 1 Cor. 12, 3b-7. 12-13; John 20, 12-23) Pentecost is one of the three most important feasts of the Church year. We know Christmas is one of the three. It's easy to get excited about the birth of a baby, especially when the baby is God's Son and his mother is the Virgin Mary. We know the feast of Jesus' resurrection is the most important feast of all, because if there were no resurrection, we would have no faith or hope at all. But Pentecost, the third most important feast, seems like another ordinary Sunday.

Let me give you a little history of Pentecost. It was not invented by the Church. The Jews were celebrating Pentecost 3000 years ago. It was one of their three most important feasts. It was originally a harvest feast on which the first fruits were offered in gratitude to God. It later came to be celebrated as the anniversary of the giving of the Law to Moses on Mt. Sinai. The word itself means simply 50th, the 50th day after Jewish Passover. The Jews were celebrating that feast when the Spirit came on Jesus' followers. And so Pentecost is still celebrated, but we who are Christians celebrate it as the day on which God sent his Holy Spirit upon the Church.

Pentecost isn't just the celebration of a past event. It is important for us today, because the Holy Spirit is important for us today. The Spirit is hard to picture because the Spirit is within us when we are in God's grace. The Spirit is like the air we breathe, the light that goes on when we have an idea, the fire that burns in our heart. And so the Scriptures use these symbols help us know the Spirit; in the first reading the Spirit is a strong driving wind whereas in John's gospel the Spirit is the gentle breath of Jesus who breathes on his apostles and says "Receive the Holy Spirit." In either case, whether as a powerful wind or a gentle breath, the Spirit is like the invisible air we cannot live without. The Spirit is like the light that goes on in our mind when we have an idea: Jesus tells us in the gospel "he will guide you to all truth." Jesus couldn't explain everything to the apostles that he wanted them to know, but the Spirit turned on the light in their minds to be able to understand all that he had been teaching them. The Spirit also appeared to the apostles as tongues of fire, a fire that started burning in them to proclaim Christ with courage and conviction.

God wants us to know him and love him and the Spirit helps us to do that. But because the Spirit works within us, we are not aware the Spirit is even there. I would like to share with you some thoughts from C.S. Lewis about how we grow in knowledge things, people and God. If we want to know something about rocks, for example, we go and we find rocks. They won't come to us, they won't run away from us. In no way do they cooperate with us in getting to know them. The initiative is all on our side if we are to know rocks. If we want to study wild animals, that's a little different. We have to go find them and if we're not really quiet they probably will run away from us (or eat us alive). The initiative is mostly on our part if we are to know about wild animals, but they could prevent us from knowing them. If we want to know another human being, and they are determined for us not to know them, we probably won't. We have to win their confidence if they are going to open up to us. The initiative is equally divided: it takes two to make a friendship. When it comes to God, there is no way we could find him or know him if he didn't show himself to us. And he has done so in Jesus Christ. But we cannot not know Jesus Christ without the help of the Spirit. As Paul tells us in today's second reading: "No one can say Jesus is Lord except in the Holy Spirit." Without the Spirit God is totally unknown to us. The Spirit makes the Scriptures alive for us and helps us to be aware of God's presence with us and God's love for us.

When we have this kind of a relationship with God it spills over into everything else we do. So St. Paul tells us in Galatians: if we live by the Spirit, the Spirit will produce in us love, joy, peace, patience, kindness, goodness, faithfulness, humility, and self-control." Most of us also are familiar with Paul's description of the greatest gift of the Spirit: "I may be able to speak the languages of men and even angels, but if have not love, my speech is no more than a noisy gong or a clanging bell...Love is patient and kind, love is not jealous, etc, etc.

One last point: it was on the Church, that God sent his Spirit. As the first reading tells us Christ followers were all together in one place. The Spirit gives different gifts to different members of the Church so we can help each other to know and experience God and God's love. If we want to experience the fullness of the Spirit, we need each other, we need to come together, to worship together, to share our gifts with one another. Without the Spirit we are trying to breathe without air, think without light, love without fire.

Feast of the Holy Trinity
June 3, 2007

INTRODUCTION – (Prov 8:22-31; Rom 5:1-5; John 16:12-15) There are a number of books in the Old Testament which are called wisdom books. Topics range from very philosophical, such as understanding the meaning of life or the meaning of suffering to very practical suggestions as to how to raise children or how to handle your money. Our first reading comes from one of the books in the wisdom tradition: the book of Proverbs. Wisdom is personified, and in today's first reading she is described as existing before creation. This personification of Wisdom is a kind of vague foreshadowing of the Trinity. Of course, the Old

Testament knew nothing of the Trinity, but what is said of wisdom could be said about both Jesus and the Holy Spirit for it is through both Jesus and the Holy Spirit that God's wisdom is revealed to us.

HOMILY – Life has many mysteries. Science tries to solve many of them and it's interesting that as we come to understand some mysteries, we discover even more. Understanding people is similar. Sometimes we don't even understand people we live with. Sometimes we don't even understand ourselves. Yet there are those who think they should understand the one who created all this mystery and that God should not be mysterious at all. There is much more in life and about God that we must learn and understand. Jesus told us that in today's gospel when he said "I have much more to tell you, but you cannot handle it now." He would send the "Spirit of truth" to guide us.

Like all mysteries in the universe, the mystery of God is something we keep understanding with greater clarity, yet we know there's much more we have to learn. The mystery of the Trinity is a reminder to us that God is greater than we can ever know. At the same time it is an invitation to continuously come to know God better. The more we know God, the more we will say we have an awesome God. Those who say there is no God, or that God cannot be known, have already closed out the possibility of finding any joy in getting to know God at all.

The mystery of the Trinity is a fundamental mystery of our faith. We were baptized into the Trinity. We begin our prayers in the name of the Trinity: the Father and the Son and the Holy Spirit. Our faith in Jesus' divinity rests on the doctrine of the Trinity. What makes the Mass unique and such a powerful prayer is that Jesus prays with us in the Mass; our prayer is offered to the

Father in union with the perfect sacrifice of Jesus through the power of the Spirit.

One of the keys to help us understand the Trinity just a little better is the concept of relationships. Without relationships in our lives, life would be unbearable. Our relationships unite us with others and yet we know we are separate from them. We are one with them yet we have our own individual lives.

When two people fall in love, there is an illusion of complete oneness. They feel a unity and completeness like they've never felt before. That's why it's such a powerful feeling. But the experience is only temporary. After a while a loving couple discovers they don't hold all things in common. Boundaries start to reappear. Where before everything was "we" and "ours," now there is also "mine" and "yours." But that is normal. That doesn't mean they no longer love each other. It only means no human being can fully satisfy us or fulfill us. Only God can.

Where does the Trinity fit in here? Well, in the Trinity, there are three persons. They are in such intense relationship with one another that, although they are distinct persons, they are so perfectly united in every way that they are one. There are no boundaries; there is nothing that separates them, except they are not the same person. There are no "mine" and "yours." As we hear Jesus say in today's gospel: "Everything that the Father has is mine." The Holy Spirit will take what is Christ's and declare it to his disciples. Everything that belongs to the one belongs to the other, yet each is not the same as the other. The only exception it seems is that the Second Person of the Trinity took on a human nature, but that is a mystery to contemplate at some other time.

If good, healthy, love filled relationships bring us joy, what joy there must be in God among the Father, the Son and the Holy Spirit! This joy is so abundant it overflows; it overflows to such an extent that God wants to share God's joy with us. This relationship between Father, Son and Spirit is what God invites us to be part of. This is grace. God loves you and God loves me, so much so that God shares God's very being with us. We probably will never understand why God loves us so much or why God chose to make us children of God. That too is a mystery, a mystery we will experience in a most wonderful way when that life of grace comes to full maturity in heavenly glory. This is why it is so important to remain in God's grace in this life, for grace is the beginning of eternal life right now.

The Body and Blood of Christ
June 10, 2007

INTRODUCTION – (Gen 14:18-20; 1 Cor 11:23-26; Luke 9:11b-17) Today we celebrate our faith in the Eucharist as the Body and Blood of our Lord, Jesus Christ. Today's first reading takes us back about 1850 years before Christ. Abraham's nephew Lot had been captured by some local tribes and Abraham set out to rescue him, which he did. On his return, he passed by Salem, which is Jerusalem today and he was met by Melchizedek, who was both king and high priest in that area. They didn't believe in separation of church and state in those early days and it was not unusual for the same person to be both king and high priest. Melchizedek offered bread and wine to Abraham. This act of eating together signified the creation of a bond of enduring friendship and mutual protection. Many of the early fathers in the Church saw this gesture as a foreshadowing of the Eucharist.

St. Paul describes the institution of the Eucharist in his letter to the Corinthians. The language he uses indicates that this is a tradition that is authentic and reliable. He received it from the Lord and he is handing it on to the Corinthians as he has received it. Receiving it "from the Lord" does not necessarily mean that he received it directly, but that it is an essential part of the gospel that has its origin in the teaching and the life of Jesus Christ.

HOMILY – I want to begin by saying to all of our fathers here: "Happy Father's Day." I was trying to find a joke about fathers and you know what, there aren't very many. There must be ten times as many jokes about mothers as there are about fathers. Perhaps fathers aren't as funny or perhaps men write most of the jokes. But since I couldn't find one about fathers I decided to tell one about mothers. There was this young son who phoned is mother and asked how she was. She said she was awfully weak. Concerned, he asked why she was so weak and she said she hadn't had anything to eat for 32 days. He was alarmed and asked what was going on she hadn't eaten for 32 days. She said it was because she didn't want to have a mouth full of food in case he would call. How's that for giving someone a guilt trip? Well, in case your mother or father are still alive and you haven't called yours recently, give them a call today. Remember fathers need love and affection as much as mothers do. They just try to be tough and don't say they do.

I was thinking fathers (and mothers) sometimes have a difficult job. They have to try to convince their children that vegetables do them more good than ice cream, that turning off the TV and going to bed early is important, especially on school nights, that they need to brush their teeth, go to school, be nice to others, share their things, do their chores and do dozens of other things that children are not inclined to do.

God the Father has the same difficult job. He tries to convince us that we are going to be happiest when we do what he tells us to do. One of the hard things he has to do, is to try to get us to to take on faith many things we cannot see. He wants us to believe in him, to believe in his love (even though we do not see it at times), to believe in his Son Jesus, to believe that death is not the end of life but for those who faithfully follow Jesus but it is the beginning of eternal life. One of the things we cannot see but have to take on faith is the Eucharist.

We heard in today's gospel the one miracle, other than the resurrection of Jesus, that is reported in all four gospels. It wasn't necessarily mentioned by all four because it was the most spectacular of Jesus miracles, but because it foreshadows the ongoing miracle of the Eucharist through which Jesus continues to feed his people with his own Body and Blood.

When a child who is told to eat spinach and carrots instead of ice cream or cake which they might prefer, they may not see benefit in doing that. We may not see anything special about this small wafer and sip from a cup that we receive in Communion. We just have to take it on faith, a faith that is founded on one thing: the very clear words of our Lord: "This is my Body" and "This is my Blood." "Do this in remembrance of me."

I was encouraged recently when I read in the Catholic Telegraph that a recent study reported that 91% of young Catholics (ages 20-39) believe the bread and wine become the Body and Blood of Christ at Mass. But I was sorry to see in the same report that only 77% say they can be a good Catholic without attending church every Sunday. It's like saying I believe that a healthy diet and exercise are really important, but I can be healthy without it.

Most of us nourish our bodies three or more times a day. Yet we're going to have to leave that part of us behind some day. What are we doing to nourish the spiritual part of us, the part of us that will live forever? Christ gives us himself because he knows we need him. "Unless you eat the flesh of the Son of Man and drink his blood, you do not have life within you." Jesus lost a lot of his followers because of that line. But he didn't back down on what he said. The Church tells us to be a good Catholic we must come to Mass at least once a week. This is the way we Catholics observe the third commandment to keep holy the Lord's day. The Church encourages our full participation at Mass, which includes the reception of Communion but says we must receive the Eucharist at least once a year to be in good standing.

When we were young and didn't feel like eating our vegetables we did it because we had to. Hopefully as we matured we got to the point that we saw the value of a good diet and followed it. So the Church makes rules about Mass and about the Eucharist to help us when we don't feel like doing what is beneficial for us, but hopefully most of us have gotten beyond that point to where we are able to be nourished in faith and joy by the bread of life and the cup of eternal salvation.

11th Sunday in Ordinary Time
June 17, 2007

HOMILY – (2 Sam 12:7-10, 13; Gal 2:16, 19-21; Luke 7:36-8:3) I hope you will pardon me if I tell a couple of cute stories for Fathers' Day.

There was a priest named O'Reilly who ran into Mrs. Donovan whom he had married to Mr. Donovan years before. Fr. O'Reilly asked how they were doing and she said fine, except for a very sad part of their life. They couldn't have children. Fr. O'Reilly said he was on his way to Rome and would light a candle for them so God would bless them with children. Several years later, Fr. O'Reilly ran into Mrs. Donovan and asked how things were going and asked if they had any children yet. She said yes, God blessed them with ten children, including three sets of twins. Fr. O'Reilly said, "praise the Lord." And how is Mr. Donovan doing and where is he now. She said, "he just left for Rome to blow out that darned candle."

Someone wrote a story of why God created children (and in the process grandchildren). Whenever your children are not perfect, take comfort in the fact that even the omnipotent God was not 100% successful with his children. He made Adam and Eve, and one of the first things he said was "DON'T." "Don't what?" Adam asked. "Don't eat the forbidden fruit!" God said. "Forbidden fruit! We have forbidden fruit? Hey Eve, we have forbidden fruit." "No way!" "Yeah, for real." "Do NOT eat the fruit" God said. "Why?" "Because I am your father and I said so!" God replied, wondering why he hadn't stopped creation after making the elephants. A few minutes later, God saw his children having an apple break and he wasn't happy. "Didn't I tell you not to eat the fruit?" God asked. "Uh huh," Adam replied. "Then why did you?" said the Father. "I don't know" said Eve. "She started it!" said Adam. "Did not!" "Did too!" "DID NOT!" Having had it with the two of them, God's punishment was that Adam and Eve should have children of their own. Thus the pattern was set and it has never changed. If you have persistently and lovingly tried to give children wisdom and they haven't taken it, don't be too hard on yourself. If God had trouble raising children, what makes you think it would be a piece of cake for you?

Things to reflect on:

§ Grandchildren are God's reward for not killing your own.

§ The main purpose of holding children's parties is to remind yourself that there are children more awful than your own.

§ Advice for the day: Be nice to your kids. They will choose your nursing home one day.

§ And finally if you have a lot of tension and you get a headache, do what it says on the aspirin bottle. "Take two aspirin" and "keep away from children."

I hope that was not too irreverent. Seriously, children are a wonderful gift and they are our future. But sometimes they can be a challenge, so I admire all parents these days who are doing the best they can with their children. I especially wish all of our fathers a very blessed and happy father's day.

I've said some of this before and if you've already heard it, please forgive me. I had a wonderful father. He was religious, he was intelligent, he was generous, he inspired his five children to work hard to use their gifts as best they could. He worked hard to provide for all of us, yet he had his faults. He did not readily forgive people who offended him, he was a dictator at home (affectionately nicknamed by my friends "the czar") and he was an alcoholic who at times did not hesitate to use his physical strength to keep law and order in the home. And he was strong. It's been 27 years since he died. For a long time I held a lot of resentment toward him, until one day the Lord relieved me of all my bad feelings. Our

Lord helped me see the kind of dysfunctional, alcoholic home my dad came from and I realized he achieved a lot with what he had to work with. When my resentment was gone, I could respect him and appreciate him for who he was and for what he had been able to make of himself. Sometimes we forget parents are human and they are the product of the environment they grew up in. Our Lord also did another favor for me. He taught me that instead of being angry about the past and blaming my parents for their faults, I should put my energy toward working on some of my own problems. Having grown up in an alcoholic home, I realized I had much to learn about forgiveness and learn how to deal with conflict in constructive ways. If we let Our Lord guide us, he will. I have a lot of positive feelings for my dad for, in spite of his faults, he was generally a very good father. I am grateful for all the good things he did for me.

A lady (not from around here) came to me recently with some marriage problems. One of her problems was that her husband had grown up in an alcoholic home. It had affected him significantly, but he was in denial (as many times alcoholics and their families are). There are serious problems in today's society where many fathers have abandoned their position of leadership in the family or they walk away from their responsibilities and aren't there at all. I read recently that the average father spends 37 seconds per day with his children according to a Cornell University study. Husbands and fathers should not think they have to act like the czar, but they have responsibilities they share with their wives to love God, and each other and to teach their children how to live good lives.

As we think of fathers, we can't forget the One who created all of us. Of course the God we call Father has no gender for God does not have a physical body. Only

Jesus does. However, the image of God as Father is a convenient and comfortable way of thinking of God for it was the way Jesus most often referred to God when he called him "abba", an Aramaic word meaning "daddy." The late Johnny Hart, who drew the cartoon BC, occasionally indulged in poetry. He wrote a poem for fathers' day that you might enjoy:

Everybody don't all have a father.

Some, there are, whose dads have passed along.

Then there's some who couldn't give less bother,

to family situations woebegone.

With dads you cannot just reach and 'nab' one,

but if for some reason you don't have one,

there's one on duty, all the time — up there!

Through our Mass today we seek to give love to our heavenly Father who loves us infinitely. We ask his help for whatever we need. As always at Mass, we join with Jesus, the perfect human being and Son of God to offer our praise, our thanks, our whole selves to the One who has given us all that we have and hope to have.

Birth of John the Baptist
June 24, 2007

INTRODUCTION – We are mostly familiar with John the Baptist from the readings during Advent, as John was the prophet who immediately preceded Jesus and foretold his coming. His birthday is June 24, which usually falls on a weekday. It is considered an important feast, so important in fact that when it falls on Sunday, it takes precedence over the Sunday readings. For those who like to follow the readings in the red Worship book, they are 1038 (eve) or 1039 (day). If you are curious why the feast of his birth is today, consider this. When the archangel Gabriel appeared to Mary, the archangel told her that her cousin Elizabeth was already in her sixth month. The church figured that John's birth had to have been six months before the birth of Jesus. So, Christmas is six months away.

The liturgy usually puts the feast days of saints on the day they died and entered into eternal life. Only three birthdays are celebrated: John the Baptist, Mary the mother of Jesus and Jesus himself. This is because their birth is considered especially holy since they were born free from any sin.

[at 4:00 (Vigil)] (Jer 1:4-10; Luke 1:5-17)

Our first reading is from Jeremiah, a prophet who lived 600 years before Christ. The reading describes the role of a prophet as was John the Baptist. It is a fitting description of John.

The gospel is the annunciation to John's father, the old priest Zechariah, that he and his elderly wife would have a child, a special child who would prepare God's people for the coming of the Messiah.

[at 8:00 and 10:00] (Isa 49:1-6; Luke 1:57-66, 80)

In today's first reading, the prophet Second Isaiah, who lived about 500 years before Christ, speaks of some mysterious person who was identified simply as God's servant. This poem and three others in Isaiah's writings are known as Servant Songs. The early Church found these songs described Jesus in a most uncanny way. They are usually read during Holy Week. Today, however, the liturgy applies this second of the Servant Songs to John the Baptist because it states: "the Lord called me from birth, from my mother's womb he gave me my name."

When the archangel Gabriel had appeared to John's father Zachariah nine months earlier, he told him his wife Elizabeth would have a son and he was to be named John. Zachariah and Elizabeth were an older couple and Zachariah didn't believe the angel. Not smart! He lost the ability to speak because of his lack of faith. (It's like the angel would not allow him to speak out his doubts but to keep his lack of faith to himself.) We hear in the gospel how Zachariah's ability to speak returned once John was born.

HOMILY – Since I gave a long introduction, I do not have a very long sermon. Or as Henry VIII said to his third wife, "I will not keep you long." One of Aesop's most famous fables is the story of the ant and the grasshopper.

The story goes like this:

In a field one summer's day a Grasshopper was hopping about, chirping and singing to its heart's content. An Ant passed by, bearing along with great toil a kernel of corn he was taking to the nest. "Why not come and chat with me," said the Grasshopper, "instead of toiling and moiling in that way?" "I am helping to lay up food for the winter," said the Ant, "and recommend you to do the same." "Why bother about winter?" said the Grasshopper; we have got plenty of food at present." But the Ant went on its way and continued its toil. When the winter came the Grasshopper had no food and found itself dying of hunger, while it saw the ants distributing every day corn and grain from the stores they had collected in the summer. Then the Grasshopper knew: "It is best to prepare for the days of necessity."

Solid, practical, down to earth wisdom from 2500 years ago! It's still true. If we do not learn this lesson when life is good, we'll regretfully learn it when it's too late. This goes for education, investing, health and all kinds of important areas of life. John the Baptist's role in life was to insist on the need to prepare. He called people to repent and prepare for the coming of God's kingdom. His message is as important today as it ever was. There is a kind of new age theology that follows the attitude of the Grasshopper. It says don't worry. We're all going to heaven. We'll all be happy in the end. God wants all people to be saved, as St. Paul tells us, but there are abundant passages in every part of the Scriptures that warn us that salvation is not a given. There are things that are necessary for salvation and things that will prevent our salvation. The gentle, loving Jesus, who revealed to us so clearly the love of God, warned us: "The door to heaven is narrow. Work hard to get in, because many will try to enter and will not be able." (Luke 13,23) Jesus, too, like John the Baptist called us to repentance and conversion of heart. I think the most important lesson we can learn from this feast of John the Baptist is to prepare. The fact you are here today is one good sign that you understand the need to prepare. If you want some more specific ideas, the insert in today's bulletin about love of God might give you a few good ideas on how to prepare better. Amen.

Thirteenth Sunday in Ordinary Time
July 1, 2007

INTRODUCTION – (1 Kgs 19:16b, 19-21; Gal 5:1, 13-18; Luke 9:51-62) Today's gospel reading brings us to a critical point in St. Luke's gospel. St. Luke tells us at this point in his gospel that Jesus turned his face toward Jerusalem. From this point on in Luke, everything that Jesus said or did took place while he was on his way to Jerusalem. This part of Luke's gospel is referred to as the "Journey narrative." When Jesus decided to go to

Jerusalem, he knew what was ahead for him, nonetheless, he started his journey with courage and determination. He warns those who would follow him that following him would require sacrifice, and there wasn't time for second thoughts or to be indecisive.

Our first reading may seem to be a strange one, but it was chosen to correspond with the idea of total commitment to one's call. It tells about two Old Testament prophets, Elijah and Elisha. Elijah is getting old and his life is coming to an end. At God's command he chooses Elisha to replace him. Placing his mantle on Elisha's shoulders symbolized this call. Having 12 yoke of oxen to plow with would indicate that Elisha must have been a prosperous farmer. His sacrificing the animals and burning his equipment indicates a total commitment to his vocation. He broke completely with his former way of life and did not look back.

HOMILY – The gospels have one objective, to lead us to Christ. Christ has one objective, to lead us to God. And God has one objective, to bring us to eternal happiness. Today's gospel, in its desire to lead us to Christ does not picture Christ as "an easy going, do whatever you want, you're all going to get to heaven anyway" kind of person. Jesus is the most loving person who ever lived, and at the same time, when it comes to eternal life, he is a non wishy-washy, ambivalent person. With regard to salvation he is no nonsense. Some people might even consider his words hard.

Let us consider some of these hard sayings. We hear first of all about an encounter with the Samaritans. Most of us probably think of the Samaritans as nice people, because of the parable of the good Samaritan. But there was considerable animosity between the Jews and the Samaritans. A Jew could risk his life traveling through Samaria and as we see in today's gospel, Jesus is prudently sending messengers ahead of him to see if a particular town would receive him. They wouldn't. James and John were all for calling down destruction upon that town. Not only did they want bad to happen to those people, they wanted to be involved. They asked Jesus, "Do you want us to call down fire from heaven upon them?" Jesus just rebuked them and moved on. Jesus did not come to condemn but to save. He was a man of peace. You are possibly thinking, how is what Jesus said here a hard saying? Well, consider who are the Samaritans in your life, the people you would like to get rid of if you could? Can you have the same attitude as Jesus, willing to avoid vengeance, willing to forgive, looking for ways to find peace? It's not always easy.

The other two or three sayings are hard ones too. There is someone in the gospel who comes up to Jesus and wants to follow him. Jesus describes the sacrifices that might be involved, especially the sacrifice of not even having a place to call home. Those who lived in the early Church had many sacrifices to make to stay faithful to our Lord, even to the extent of maybe having to sacrifice their lives. People still do in other places of the world today. But in our country so many people find it hard to sacrifice an hour for Sunday Mass or time to pray during the week, not to mention the sacrifice involved in keeping the commandments. Being a Christian is not just a matter of saying we are. It is living the way Christ wants us to.

"Let the dead bury their dead" is one of the hardest to understand. I have always understood this as the situation of the young man who wouldn't be ready to follow Jesus until his father died which may have been years away. Jesus was saying there wouldn't be time. How many times do we say when I get this done or that done, then I'll begin going to Church more or spend more time praying? We're all busy today. Where we choose to spend our time tells us what's important to us. The devil's biggest temptation for many of us is to tell us "you have lots of time. You can pray later. You can do that good deed later. Just relax for a little while. You owe it to yourself." (Of course we need to relax at times, but we also need to make time for the Lord.)

The last statement is very similar. "No one who sets a hand to the plow and looks to what was left behind is fit for the kingdom of God." Our following Christ has to be serious. We can't be indecisive and uncommitted. We can't let feelings alone guide us, deciding to pray when we feel like it and putting our faith aside when we don't feel like it. Our faith is too important for that. I remember all the new faces I saw in church after 9/11. I'm glad people came but for many the enthusiasm didn't last. God deserves better than a passing thought or a spurt of piety when we happen to feel like it.

Hard sayings! They sure are. Are they meant to accuse us or put us down or depress us? No. Our Lord's words to us come from his love and his objective is to lead us to holiness and eternal happiness.

14th Sunday in Ordinary Time
July 8, 2007

INTRODUCTION – (Isa 66:10-14c; Gal 6:14-18; Luke 10:1-12, 17-20) Our first reading describes a time in Jewish history right after the Babylonian exile. The Jews had been returning home to Israel after they had been slaves and exiles for 50 years. Their cities, lands and homes were in ruins. Consequently, they were discouraged and depressed. God encouraged them with messages of comfort and hope through the prophet

Isaiah. He did not bring them home from exile to abandon them. Jerusalem will be like a mother once again, nurturing them and caring for them. They must rejoice. They will enjoy prosperity once again. The psalm refrain echoes this call to rejoice.

HOMILY – Only St. Luke tells us of the 72 disciples Jesus sent out. There was too much to do for the Twelve. Even today, the official leaders of the Church cannot reach all the people who need to hear God's message of love and peace. For Jesus it was quite a few more helpers he had to recruit. It seems the first thing he said to them was "there aren't even enough of you." "The harvest is abundant but the laborers are few; pray for more workers for the harvest." The next thing he did was warn them. It would be a dangerous job. They would be like lambs in the midst of wolves. That's not a very appealing image. Lambs have no defense. Their only defense is their shepherd. Of course, Jesus knew the heavenly Father would watch over them. Jesus sent them out in pairs. He knows we need each other's support in our journey of faith. Their mission probably didn't take them very far and probably not for a very long time. That's partly why they needed no money or luggage. The other reason they needed to take nothing with them was because they needed to learn to rely on God to provide for them. They had God's peace, which they could share with whoever was open to it. They had power over demons and they had the gift to heal. You would think they would have been received with open arms wherever they went and it seems as if they were. They came back to Jesus full of joy. Their mission was urgent; they weren't to stand around shooting the breeze with people, "greet no one along the way," and their message was simple. They weren't ready to preach or teach like Jesus did. They were only to tell people the kingdom of God was near.

What is the kingdom of God? We pray for it all the time: "Thy kingdom come." Jesus preached about it many times, often in parables. It is something that not all people want to be part of for it will be like a farmer's field where some of the seed is productive while some withers and dies. Or it is like a field where wheat and weeds grow together until harvest when the wheat is kept and the weeds are destroyed. But for those who open their hearts to the kingdom, it will be wonderful. It will be like a great banquet, like the wedding celebration for a prince. It will be eternal, it will be peaceful, it will be a rule of love, it will be joy beyond our ability to imagine. Because it is near, Jesus tells his 72, "rejoice, rejoice that your names are written in heaven."

I'm going to tell you a story about what heaven might be like. Old Mr. Murphy loved Ireland. He worked and toiled on its land when he was young. He poured his sweat into its soil. He raised his sons and daughters on its fertile ground. He fought for its freedom. When he could, he traveled its length and breadth. He loved it so much that when it came time to die, he had his sons carry him outside so he could lay next to the ground. He even grabbed a handful of earth to hold onto. And that's the way he died. When he got to heaven's gates God came to meet him. God had the appearance of an old man, like we're used to thinking of God the Father, white hair and beard. God told him he was a good man and welcomed him to heaven. But God said he couldn't bring that dirt into heaven. Murphy couldn't let go of it; he loved Ireland so much. So God left Murphy standing at heaven's gate and went back inside. A few years past and God came out again, this time with the appearance of one of Murphy's drinking buddies. They chatted and told a few jokes, then God invited Murphy to come on in but to let go of the dirt he was holding onto. But

Murphy couldn't; he loved Ireland so much. So God sadly left him there at heaven's gates. After more years God appeared again, this time as one of Murphy's granddaughters. She told him how everyone missed him and begged him to come in. By this time Murphy's joints had stiffened and his hands could no longer hold on to the little part of Ireland he was trying to take with him. The soil fell from his hands and God brought Murphy inside. Once inside he couldn't believe it, there before his eyes was his beloved Ireland and much more besides. Sometimes people are so enamored of the little bits and pieces of God's creation that they have a hold on that they can't believe there could be anything better. But if we open ourselves in faith to whatever God asks of us, if we open ourselves in faith to the glory that Christ promised to those who follow him, we will already begin to know God's kingdom. Then we will understand Jesus' parable that the kingdom is like a treasure buried in a field or a pearl of great price. The kingdom is something we cannot see now, but it is near for those who see it in faith. It is joy beyond imagining.

The power and presence of the risen Christ fills us when God's grace is in us, for that is what grace is: God's life. It is a life that will endure forever in peace and love. This is the good news, the gospel, this was the preaching of Jesus, the proclamation of the 72, "The Kingdom of God is near." Believe it, and in this faith and this hope, rejoice.

15th Sunday in Ordinary Time
July 15, 2007

INTRODUCTION – (Deut 30:10-14; Col 1:15-20; Luke 10:25-37) The Book of Deuteronomy is a series of sermons addressed to the people of Israel by Moses right before they were to enter the Promised Land. Moses had led them from the slavery of Egypt and was with them for many years as they traveled through the Sinai desert. You might remember Moses knew he would die before the people could enter their Promised Land, so he is in a sense giving them some last words of wisdom before he would have to leave them. Today's first reading begins with an incomplete sentence: "If only you would heed the voice of the Lord..." The sentence presupposes a thought such as: "God will bless you, if only you would heed the voice of the Lord..." The passage goes on to stress that what God wants from his people is no hidden mystery. God has been very clear as to how he wants us to live. This concept connects with today's gospel when a scholar of the law asks Jesus to interpret for him what God wants of any of us. Jesus' reply to the man's question shows that he already had the answer he was looking for. Almost instinctively, we all know what God wants of all of us. Knowing it is not the problem, but living it is.

HOMILY – I have two confessions to make. The first one is not exactly relevant to today's readings, but I thought you might enjoy it. While I was working on my sermon Friday afternoon, I was reading over old sermons I had preached in past years looking for ideas and I almost put myself to sleep. So if anyone nods off, I won't be offended.

The second confession I have to make is about Jesus' parable. In the early days of my priesthood, I didn't like to have to read this gospel. I thought it always gave priests a bad rap. Priests are supposed to be good, caring, always willing to help others. We all know, unfortunately, they are not always that way. I have to humbly confess there were times when I've been like the priest or Levite in the story. I've turned people down who were looking for help. I've been taken by all kinds of people, even people I've trusted, and I've been taken big time, and I'm not just talking about a few hundred dollars! I have to admit I've grown less trusting as I've gotten older. Love is not just a matter of reaching out to help someone, it's also a matter of how much you are willing to risk being hurt or letting someone use you or take advantage of you. I think this is one of the hard lessons in today's gospel.

You know, the Jewish man was a victim of robbers could have been dead. If so, it would have disqualified the priest and Levite from participation in Jewish worship for several days, because contact with a dead person made a Jew ritually unclean according to the Law. I remember a few years ago a rabbi doing a funeral service for a friend of mine, and the rabbi stood outside on the porch of the funeral home saying the prayers and giving the sermon. By law he could not even enter the funeral home. If the victim in Jesus' story were dead, the priest and Levite were doing what the Jewish law required of them if they were going to participate in any religious service. On the other hand, what if he were a decoy. The robbers could have been hiding nearby, waiting for someone to try to help this poor man, then they would have one more person they could pounce on. Being a good Samaritan is risky business, and that's what love is. It is risky business too. Our Lord is telling us in today's gospel love demands we sometimes stick our necks out and take the risk of being hurt or being used or taken advantage of.

When Jesus said the two greatest commandments were about love: love of God and love of neighbor, the Jewish scholar asked Jesus another question: "And who is my neighbor?" You might recall that there was great animosity between Jews and Samaritans, so in introducing a Samaritan into the story, Jesus shows us "neighbor" could be anyone, even someone we despise.

There is another question I wish the Jewish scholar had asked. I wish he had asked Jesus "And what is love." In our modern culture love is such a fuzzy concept and is equated in most people's minds with something that makes me feel good. I think if I pray and I feel good, I am loving God. If I pray and I feel as if I'm not getting anything out of it, I feel like I'm wasting my time. If I do something for someone else and I feel good, I think I've been a loving person. If I do something for someone and they don't say thanks or don't seem to appreciate it or just take me for granted, I don't feel good and decide it wasn't worth it. Modern culture has taught us to measure every loving act by our feelings, our reward, our payback. Sure sometimes we pray and feel good and sometimes we do something for someone and feel good about it. But sometimes we don't. Love is measured by what we give, (to God, worship and praise, to others what good things we do for them); it's not measured by the good we get out of what we do. The Good Samaritan may have felt good doing what he did, or he may have felt burdened by the extra stress and inconvenience this put on him. Jesus doesn't tell us how the Samaritan felt. He tells us of the good thing he did.

While we speak of the Good Samaritan, I might point out our Good Samaritan window. But our best example of love is right here at Mass. Jesus came to us and was willing to give all to save us. We were the person needing to be rescued from ignorance, sin and death and he came along as the Good Samaritan and gave his life for us. We not only have his example of love in this Eucharist, but we are united with him so that we can be empowered to love others in the same way. In our Eucharist (a Greek word which means "thanksgiving") we thank God for all he has done for us in Jesus and we ask his help to become more loving as he has taught us. Amen.

16th Sunday in Ordinary Time
July 22, 2007

INTRODUCTION – (Gen 18:1-10a; Col 1:24-28; Luke 10:38-42) One of the themes of today's readings is hospitality. Jesus, and most likely his disciples, share the hospitality of Martha and Mary, his friends in Bethany. Our first reading is about Abraham who welcomes three strangers with a lavish banquet. The Bible said he was 100 years old, but he was still pretty energetic as we hear. He doesn't realize it at the time that it is God whom he is entertaining. God must have enjoyed the feast, for God tells him that his lifelong desire that he and his wife, Sarah, would have a son would finally be fulfilled.

HOMILY – There was a man who went to see his doctor and he had a carrot sticking out of one ear and a piece of celery sticking our of the other, with a couple of grape stuck up his nose. He complained to the doctor he was not feeling well. The doctor said "It's obvious, that you're not eating properly!"

I hope you will pardon me for emphasizing the obvious, but everybody enjoys eating. Most of us sit down to eat several times a day and probably snack occasionally in-between. Jesus was away from his home territory of Galilee and was near Jerusalem when he visited Martha and Mary in Bethany. He and most likely his disciples probably hadn't had a good meal for a while and Martha was ready to put out a really fine feast for them all. But Jesus knew that in addition to feeding our bodies, there are other needs that we human beings have. After all, he is the one who responded to the temptations of the devil in the desert, after forty days of fasting, that we do not live by bread alone! Our hearts need to be fed with love and our spirits need to be fed with wisdom and truth. And Martha's sister, Mary, was needing to be fed with the wisdom and truth and love that Jesus spoke. When Jesus said "Mary has chosen the better part," was he saying that sitting and praying or reading the Bible is more important than having a good meal? I don't think so. We need both. It wouldn't be a bad idea though if sometimes we ate a little less and prayed a little more. We seldom get so busy that we forget to eat in the course of a day. How often do we forget to spend a little while with God during the course of a day or even during the course of a week. When Jesus said "Mary has chosen the better part," was he saying taking time to pray is better than feeding a hungry person? I don't think Jesus is saying that either. We need to do both. I think that's why St. Luke put this story right after the parable of the Good Samaritan. St. Luke is telling us we need balance. We need to do good things for others, but we need to take time just to sit at our Lord's feet and communicate with him. I'm sure most of us remember the passage from the Book of Qoheleth: "For everything there is a season, and a time for every matter under heaven: a time to be born, and a time to die; a time to plant, and a time to pluck up what is planted; etc." Perhaps what Jesus was saying to Martha when he said "Mary has chosen the better part," he was saying this is a golden opportunity; here is the Son of God coming to visit and you're worried about chopping up the parsley; or perhaps he was saying "you're trying to put out an eight course meal, Martha, and we would be happy with just a sandwich," or perhaps he was saying "maybe we ought to think about feeding the spirit before feeding our faces;" or perhaps he was saying "maybe we need to spend a little time enjoying each other's company before we get all uptight about dinner."

I remember some years ago when I would visit home, I just wanted to spend a little time sitting and talking and my mother was always trying to serve something to eat, even if I had just had supper. Frustrating! Now she is in a nursing home and when I visit, she's not trying to feed me. We both just enjoy the visit. On the other hand, I have heard from so many wives how their husbands never have time to sit down and talk. They're always busy doing something or else they're half asleep in front of the TV. They complain "I feel like I'm all alone." In too many families today, the family members are too busy to listen to one another, to talk to one another, to feed one another emotionally. We do not live by bread alone.

Jesus came to Martha and Mary's house and was given hospitality. Jesus did not belittle what Martha was doing. She was trying to see that Jesus and his apostles were fed. I'm sure he appreciated it. But he wanted to feed them too, with a food that would not just satisfy them for a few hours but for eternity. Didn't he tell us in another place: "Do not labor for the food which perishes, but for the food which endures to eternal life, which the Son of man will give to you?" (Jn. 6,27) As we come here today we are giving God our worship, our time, our love, our thanks, our prayer and our praise. Our being here is a gift to our God who created us and to our Savior who died for us. But we're not just giving. We sit at his feet, listening to his word, being fed with his wisdom and truth. We receive him in Communion, we open our hearts to his love and presence. We pause for moments of silence so he can speak to us. Prayer is not just doing all the talking. It is also listening. Everything has its appointed time. Now, on this Lord's day, is the appointed time to be like Mary in today's gospel and communicate with our Lord.

17th Sunday in Ordinary Time
July 29, 2007

INTRODUCTION – (Gen 18:20-32; Col 2:12-14; Luke 11:1-13) Last Sunday's first reading told us about a visit Abraham had from three strangers. It turns out one of the three visitors was God himself. God was on his way to two cities near the Dead Sea, Sodom and Gomorrah, and he invited Abraham to go with him. On the way God took Abraham into his confidence and told him the cities were about to be destroyed because of their depravity and immorality. Notice the comfortable yet respectful familiarity that existed between God and Abraham.

HOMILY – A young minister was asked to say prayers at a burial. He was told it was a homeless person and they were being laid to rest in a little country cemetery in which no one else had yet been buried. He got lost on the way there. By the time he arrived, he saw the backhoe, there were three or four workers eating lunch and the hole was half filled, but there was no funeral director in sight. He knew he was really late and he was totally embarrassed. He apologized profusely to the workers, stepped up to the graveside and started to pray. The workers joined in with Alleluia's and Amen's and Praise the Lord. The young minister preached enthusiastically for quite a while from several scripture passages. He closed his prayer book and went back to his car. As he neared his car he heard one of the workers say: "I ain't never seen anything like that before and I've been putting in septic tanks for 20 years."

We can pray anytime, you know. I'll bet that septic tank worked perfectly for 200 years! I will say later, no prayer is ever wasted, but sometimes prayer is more fitting than at other times. It is a curious request the apostles brought to Jesus, asking him how to pray. These were not guys who suddenly got religion. Some of them may have been, but some of them had previously been disciples of John the Baptist. Surely John taught them how to pray. Being Jews, they would have gone to synagogue every Sabbath for that was a must for all Jews. There they would have heard two readings from the "Old Testament," and they would have heard two sermons, one for each of the readings. They would have prayed and sung psalms too. Jews prayed the psalms as part of their daily prayers as well. Yet they ask our Lord, "teach us to pray." It could be that the apostles observed Jesus at prayer and they knew there must be something more. Jesus' response gave them some insight into his own personal communication with the Father. St. Luke's version of the Lord's Prayer is a little shorter than the version we find in St. Matthew but essentially the same. St. Matthew's is the one we are familiar with.

Mostly whenever we think of prayer we think of asking for things. When we are in need of God's help, it is appropriate to ask for it. Yet there is a more important reason to pray than simply to tell God we need something. The more important reason is to build a relationship with God. Relationships cannot exist without communication. We could safely say the quality of our relationship with someone depends on the quality of our communication with them. Because the ability to communicate is something we have to learn, hundreds of books are written to help us improve our skill in that area. We need to learn how to communicate with God, just as we need to learn how to communicate with one another. Because God is infinitely greater than we are, communication with God is more difficult. If prayer came so easily, our church would be filled every week! Even with the Third Commandment that tells us we have an obligation to worship God, people find the slightest reason to avoid putting time aside for God.

Jesus knows prayer has its difficulties. That's why he tells us not to give up. There are lots of people who get religious only when they want something. When they pray and don't get what they ask for, they are further convinced that prayer doesn't work. Jesus, on the other hand, tells us it does. The problem is we get too impatient and we want things right away. Too often when we pray we forget our prayers are addressed to "our Father." As we know, sometimes fathers say "no" or "not yet" or "I don't think that would be a good idea." Notice also Jesus tells us before we start asking for things we first say "thy will be done."

Prayer is an expression of our faith. That's partly why prayer is not easy, because faith is not easy. When we enter into prayer, we are entering into a dialogue as Abraham did. We tell God what we would like, yet at the same time we recognize God is the one who has the last word, not us. What is that last word? It is our eternal happiness. That will be the kingdom he wants us to be part of and he will not give us anything that may get in the way of our being part of his kingdom. He even tells us to pray for it. "Thy kingdom come."

Jesus said, "Ask and you will receive." He doesn't say, "you might receive or maybe you'll receive, but you will receive." What he is saying is that no prayer is wasted. Prayer cannot fail to bring some blessing – even if it's not the thing we think we need most. If we truly believe God is all wise and all loving, then we have to conclude that if we do not receive what we've asked for, God has something better in mind. This is partly why people give up on prayer, they do not have this faith in God's wisdom and love. Prayer works, even when we do not see immediate results.

I think it is important to say a word about distractions. So many people get discouraged when they pray. I've quoted Thomas Merton before. He said, if you don't get distracted during prayer, you're brain dead. It's good to remember that distractions are normal. I believe whenever we even try to pray, God is pleased that we are reaching out to him. One of the easiest ways the devil has to lead us away from God is to discourage us or to convince us not to pray. He tells us "it doesn't work," "you're wasting your time," "it's boring," "you have too many other things to do," "you're too tired now," etc, etc. Don't ever quit praying, no matter what. It will always bring you great blessings and most important, it will bring you to a deeper relationship with God. Now we pray the greatest prayer there is, the prayer Jesus gave us at the Last Supper, the Eucharist.

18th Sunday in Ordinary Time
August 5, 2007

INTRODUCTION – (Eccl 1:2, 2:21-23; Col 3:1-5, 9-11; Luke 12:13-21) Today's first reading comes from one of the wisdom books in the Old Testament. This book is sometimes called by its Hebrew title, Qoheleth. The name means simply "one who convenes an assembly." The author was probably a teacher or preacher. When the name Qoheleth is translated into the Greek, it comes out Ecclesiastes. It's a book we hear from only once in the three-year Sunday cycle of readings. And it's a short passage at that. Most of us are familiar with another passage in Qoheleth that begins: "For everything there is a season...a time for every matter under heaven. A time to be born and a time to die, and so on...." Today's passage reminds us of the passing nature of all things.

HOMILY – A sign outside of church announced: "Don't wait for the hearse to take you to church." Today's gospel shows us the folly of failing to grow rich spiritually. It's the only thing that's will outlast everything else. Billy Graham once pointed out "You never see a hearse pulling a U-Haul trailer." When the richest man in a town died, the local news reporter asked his pastor, "how much did he leave." The pastor replied, "All of it!"

Qoheleth said "All things are vanity." The Hebrew word used here for "vanity" means something without substance, something like a puff of smoke. If you read the book of Qoheleth, you get the impression that the author enjoyed all the best things life had to offer: pleasure, wealth, power and knowledge. Yet he found nothing of lasting value or satisfaction. The conclusion of this book tells us to enjoy each day as it comes and not become too attached to anything this world has to offer. It was a practical way of looking at life considering Jewish faith at this time in history had not yet come to a faith in the existence of heaven or hell, reward or punishment. They believed in a kind of existence after death, but it was an existence that was neither happy nor unhappy. With whatever information he had, Qoheleth's conclusion to just enjoy each day as it comes was the best idea anyone could come up with.

But Jesus has more to offer. Jesus offers us something that is lasting. Jesus called the rich farmer a "fool" in today's parable, because the farmer thought he was set for life, he had all he needed. He was wealthy in worldly goods but he did not grow rich in the sight of God. The word "fool" here means someone with limited thinking, someone without good sense! St. Paul gives us the same message in today's second reading: "Think of what is above, not of what is on earth."

The parable Jesus gives us follows a few comments he made about greed and how dangerous it is. Greed certainly is dangerous. It is one of the capital sins and gives rise to things like cheating, stealing, lying, quarreling, fighting and even war. It doesn't sound as if the farmer did any of these bad things. It sounds as if he made his fortune by good weather and good old fashioned hard work. Is Jesus saying it is sinful to be rich and successful? Jesus seems to be saying it is a sin if that is our main focus in life, if we build our security only on the things this world can give us, if we forget where our blessings come from. It is also a sin to be rich if our hearts are cold to the sufferings of those not so fortunate as we are. I'm not trying to make anyone here feel guilty about not giving a buck to every bum who asks for it. I don't do that myself and I don't feel guilty about it, because I know, from past experience, most of the people who got money out of me were just con artists. I tend to let legitimate agencies, which I support, help the really poor. Going back to the rich farmer, he forgot he was not in control. He owned so much he thought he owned the future and he didn't. He didn't know he had no future and all his wealth would be left behind. His priorities were wrong, Jesus said. There are two remedies that help us keep our priorities in balance. First of all there is the third commandment, which tells us to keep holy the Lord's day. Honoring God reminds us of who God is and that we owe God everything we have and everything we are. Secondly there's a remedy to help us not forget about the needs of others. It's called tithing. Giving away some of our money reminds us it's not all ours. (10% was required of the Jewish people.) It keeps us aware that what we have has been given to us in the first place. People like to say, "I earned it." Maybe so, but where did we get the health, the talent, the energy, the education, the opportunities to earn it. That was all given to us. We do have to provide for ourselves and our families and we have to save for that proverbial rainy day, but we can't become totally selfish either. That's greed. We have to keep things in balance and loving God and loving our neighbor is part of the balance.

You've heard this story before, but it's worth repeating. An American tourist, traveling in Europe, paid a visit to a famous wise and holy rabbi who lived there. The American was surprised when he saw how simply the man lived – in a single room with only books and a table and chair. "Rabbi! Where is your furniture?" asked the tourist. "Where is yours?" the rabbi asked. The American tourist answered, "My furniture? I'm only passing through here." The wise rabbi responded: "So am I!"

19th Sunday in Ordinary Time
August 12, 2007

INTRODUCTION – (Wis 18:6-9; Heb 11:1-2, 8-19; Luke 12:32-48) The spiritual tradition we follow as Christians did not begin with Christ. It began long before Christ as God prepared the world for the coming of Christ through the Jewish people. Our two readings take us back in history to our spiritual beginning. Today's second reading takes us back to the time of Abraham, almost 19 centuries before Christ. Abraham and his wife Sarah were the parents of the Jewish people. The letter to the Hebrews puts Abraham and Sarah before us as models of faith for us to imitate. The first reading takes us several centuries after the time of Abraham to the time when God's people, in faith, left Egypt to head for the Promised Land under the leadership of Moses.

HOMILY – We were introduced to the faith of Abraham and Sarah as they left their homeland and relatives to travel to a new land where God was leading them. They had faith too in God's promise they would have many descendants even as they were without children and were growing older. We were introduced to the faith of the Jewish people as they set out under the leadership of Moses, leaving behind an unpleasant life of slavery for a more uncertain journey through desert and wilderness to an unknown land.

Each of us today is making his or her own journey. It might be toward graduation from school, it might be toward marriage or toward a new career, it might be toward improved health, it might be toward retirement or it might be just a matter of trying to survive the stresses of each day. Whatever it is, time is moving us along. We are unable to stand still in life, and if we try, we'll eventually discover that we're going backwards. We know from everyday experience that if it's a better place we are moving toward, we need to adequately prepare ourselves for it.

In our journey through life, there is an event that we definitely need to prepare for. That is the day we are going to meet our Lord, not just in prayer, not just in the sacraments, not just in the invisible ways in which he comes into our lives, but in a visible, unmistakable way at the end of life's journey through this life. It's a meeting most of us like to put off as long as possible and many people do not like to even think about. That's why our Lord warns us to prepare for it, because we may tend to procrastinate or just put it out of our minds altogether.

Jesus uses two simple examples. The first is about the head of a household who was out of town for a wedding celebration. In Jesus' day wedding celebrations often went on for days, so it's understandable that the servants would not know when to expect their master's return. The second is about a thief. Of course, a thief doesn't warn a person before breaking into their house. If Jesus were preaching today, he might use the example of terrorism. We're sadly familiar with the havoc it can cause and the need to be diligently on the alert. Unlike a thief or a terrorist who may be prevented from striking, Jesus' coming is not a matter of if but of when.

The reason he warns us is not to fill us with fear, but because he loves us and he wants us to share in all the blessings he has for us. If we're not ready, we may miss out. Most of God's people who left Egypt started off with faith, but when the going got difficult they refused to do the things God told them and they missed out on enjoying the blessings of the Promised Land.

I am sure many people here have seen the sign which said, "Jesus is coming. Try to look busy!" Being prepared is not something we can fake or make happen at the last second. It's the way we live our lives in faith and love. Faith and love are not superficial attitudes that have no substance. They are attitudes that guide us to live our life every day the way Jesus taught us.

Right now we follow the lead Jesus gave us as we do in his memory what he commanded us, worshipping the Father through our sharing in his perfect sacrifice. Amen.

Feast of the Assumption - Vigil Mass
August 14, 2007

INTRODUCTION AT THE VIGIL – It is a dogma of our faith that at the end of her life, Mary, like her son, was taken body and soul into heavenly glory. This is the meaning of the Assumption, whose vigil we celebrate this evening.

Our first reading (I Chronicles 15, 3-4,15-16; 16, 1-2) is about the Ark of the Covenant, the sacred gold plated box that contained the Ten Commandments. The Ark was the unique symbol of God's presence with Israel. It was constructed in the desert by Moses on the way to the Promised Land. When King David established his capital in Jerusalem about the year 1000 BC, he brought the Ark there. Today's reading describes this solemn and joyful occasion. After the temple was built, the Ark was placed in the Holy of Holies and there it remained for 400 years until the Babylonians destroyed the temple and took the Ark. The Babylonians may have destroyed it or it may be hidden away somewhere, but so far Indiana Jones hasn't found it!

In Christian symbolism, Mary is sometimes referred to as the Ark of the Covenant. Just as God was present in a special way wherever the Ark was taken, so God was present with Mary in a most special way when she carried within her womb the only Son of God, Jesus our Savior.

The early Christians also saw Jerusalem as a symbol of heaven. That symbolism is reflected in today's first reading. The Ark being taken up to Jerusalem symbolizes Mary being taken body and soul into the heavenly kingdom.

HOMILY – A woman in today's gospel exclaimed how fortunate Jesus' mother was to have had such a son. (Lk. 11, 27-28) On first hearing Jesus' response it sounds as if Jesus is denying the importance of his mother. Jesus was saying, however, that the most important thing about Mary is not her physical motherhood, but it was her willingness to do all that God asked of her. That made her more one with Jesus and more like Jesus than anything else. She was the perfect and number one disciple of Jesus in always being willing to do what God asked of her. She remained faithful during even her most bitter trials and challenging moments.

In our society a person's importance is usually defined by wealth or fame. With God it's not that way. It's our relationship with Jesus and our willingness to love God and others as he did. And Mary was absolutely the best in this regard, so much so that she was first to share in the fullness of life Christ came to bring us, which includes the resurrection of our bodies.

Today's feast is a feast to honor Mary and it is fitting that we do so, since God himself has so honored her. But it is also a feast that shows us God's plans for all those who faithfully follow God's will.

Feast of the Assumption
August 15, 2007

INTRODUCTION ON THE FEAST – (Rev. 11, 19a; 12, 1-6a, 10ab; I Cor. 15, 20-27; Lk. 1, 39-56) The book of Revelation is highly symbolic. Some of the symbolism is quite obvious while it requires a fairly extensive knowledge of Scripture to interpret some of the other symbols. In today's first reading we hear about a woman, a child and a dragon. The dragon is the devil and the powers of evil at work in the world. The child is Christ. The woman in our reading has a double symbolism. She stands for Mary, the physical mother of Jesus Christ, and she stands for the Church, our spiritual mother who brings Jesus Christ to birth in us through faith and the sacraments. In today's passage the woman is rescued from the powers of the dragon and is described in great glory. This too has a double symbolism. It symbolizes the glory of Mary in the assumption. It also symbolizes God's faithful people whom he will rescue from evil and will bring, in the resurrection from the dead, into the glory of heaven.

HOMILY – It is recorded nowhere in Scripture when, where or how Mary died. Nor do the Scriptures tell us about her assumption. It has been a part, however, of the very ancient tradition of the Church that Mary was assumed bodily into heavenly glory when her life here on earth was ended. One early document referring to this event comes from the Bishop of Jerusalem in 451, St. Juvenal. He was asked by the emperor of Constantinople to bring the body of Mary to Constantinople. He replied to the emperor that Mary had died in the presence of all the apostles. But her tomb, when opened upon the request of St. Thomas, was found empty. Thus the apostles concluded that her body was taken up to heaven as Jesus was.

Some people belittle tradition as if it were unimportant. They claim to believe only the written words of the Scriptures. Yet, if we stop and think about it, we would have no Scriptures without tradition for the Scriptures came from the Church's tradition. For example, the earliest New Testament writings we have are the letters of Paul, the first of which was written about the year 51 A.D. Of our four gospels, Mark's is the first and it was written about 70 A.D. I say this so you can see the importance of tradition. The Church had only its tradition to go on until Paul and the evangelists started writing it down 20, 30, 40 years after Christ, at the earliest. So to say that the knowledge of the assumption of Mary came from the very early tradition of the Church is to give a lot of weight to this teaching. But to eliminate any doubt as to whether Mary actually was assumed into heavenly glory, the Holy Father, Pope Pius XII, after reviewing the belief of the Church through the ages, made it a dogma of our faith in 1950.

In today's gospel St. Luke tells us about Mary who is a young girl going to visit her much older cousin Elizabeth. Mary had just been visited by the angel, and she had accepted the invitation to be the mother of the Savior God was sending to his people. So she is at this moment unmarried and yet pregnant through the power of the Holy Spirit It was not a happy situation to be in. She could have been rejected by her husband to be, she could have been rejected by her family or could even have been put to death. Yet she is full of trust in God and praises God's greatness and God's goodness. There is no expression of "poor me." She is entirely focused on God. Mary shows us how to be trusting and in her assumption she shows us where that trust will lead us.

Today's feast honors Mary, for God himself has honored her. In her openness to God and in her willingness to always do whatever God wanted, God rewarded her in a unique way. But today's feast also is a source of hope for us. Christ came, as he says in St. John's gospel, that we might have the fullness of life. Our faith tells us our bodies too will share in that fullness. So Mary is allowed to enjoy ahead of time what God's plan is for all of us who are faithful in following him and serving him.

20th Sunday in Ordinary Time
August 19, 2007

INTRODUCTION – (Jer 38:4-6, 8-10; Heb 12:1-4; Luke 12:49-53) Unfortunately suffering and turmoil have been part of everyday life in the Middle East for a long time. Our first reading takes us back 600 years before Christ when the land we now know as Iraq had the name Babylon. The Babylonians were in power at that time in history and the king and his army's ambitions were to conquer all the nations around them. The events in our first reading occurred at a time when the Babylonians were trying to take Jerusalem. Jeremiah, God's prophet, told the Jews it was useless for them to fight or to try to defend themselves; they should just go ahead and surrender or Jerusalem would be destroyed. Such talk was viewed as unpatriotic and Jeremiah was considered a traitor. Many of the Jewish leaders decided to kill Jeremiah and they persuaded their king, Zedekiah, to give in to their wishes. He allowed Jeremiah to be thrown into a cistern to die. Later, Ebed-Melech, a Cushite (which means an Ethiopian), one of Jeremiah's friends, persuaded the king to change his mind.

HOMILY – A "Calvin and Hobbes" cartoon pictured Calvin, the little boy sitting under a sign that read "kick in the butt for one dollar!" When Hobbes, a talking tiger and Calvin's playmate, saw his friend sitting under this sign, he asked "How's business?" "Awful!" Calvin replied, "and I don't know why, because so many people need a good kick in the butt!"

A lot of us might need it at times, but few of us appreciate it. The people who heard Jeremiah's predictions that Jerusalem would be destroyed if they didn't surrender weren't happy about what they heard. They hoped to get rid of Jeremiah as a result. Jesus too had to confront many of the people in authority in his day and we know what happened to him. Knowing how he would be rejected and would have to suffer for teaching God's message, he felt it only fair to warn his followers that they may be in for a lot of pain and suffering if they chose to follow him.

Pain and suffering, of course, comes to everyone, whether we are good, bad or indifferent. If we do not live good lives, often we have to suffer for it, but sometimes even those who are perfectly faithful to God have to suffer too, as we hear today. One of my favorite books, The Road Less Traveled, begins with a very profound insight. M. Scott Peck, a psychiatrist and Episcopal priest, begins his book by saying "Life is Difficult." That's not especially profound, but what I found so profound is his statement that once we accept life is difficult, it's not so difficult. It's more difficult for those who think it shouldn't be so. I had a good friend who was pushing a person in a wheelchair at his synagogue and while he was doing this he suffered a stroke. He would often cynically say to me "no good deed goes unpunished." I think at times we all feel that way, that life is not fair. I believe most of us have the unexpressed expectation that if we do what God wants, God should do what we want. Well, sometimes he does, and sometimes he doesn't, at least not right away.

A lot of times it's not the difficulties that come our way that cause us pain and suffering but the attitude we take toward them. Dr. Richard Carlson's book: Don't sweat the small stuff, and it's all small stuff, tells the story of a journalist interviewing two bricklayers working at a construction site. The journalist asked the one man, "what are you doing?" He said, "I'm just an underpaid and overworked bricklayer wasting my time piling bricks on top of one another." He asked the other what he was doing and he said, "I'm the luckiest person in the world. I get to be a part of great and important projects. I help turn single bricks into magnificent structures." They were both right. We see in life what we want to see. If you want to find ugliness, you will find plenty of it. If you want to find fault with life you can find lots of reasons to do so. But the opposite is also true. There are times when in my ministry and in my life, I feel like the luckiest person in the world. I am grateful that I am in a position at times to be able to help people in very important ways. On the other hand, there have been moments when I felt like Jeremiah, sinking in the mud at the bottom of a well where everything looks dark and hopeless. It's only faith that gets me through. I know God will not fail us if we are faithful to him, but God does not always make things happen the way we think he should. When he doesn't make things go our way, we have to trust God has a better plan, a plan we do not yet see. The letter to the Hebrews which we heard speaks of the example of Jesus whose work and life seemed to be a great failure when he died on a cross, but now he has taken his seat at the right hand of the throne of God. The author of the letter encourages us not to grow despondent, but to keep alive in us the hope of eternal joy that God has promised to those who are faithful to him. When we take our last breath, that is what's really going to count. Amen.

21st Sunday in Ordinary Time
August 26, 2007

INTRODUCTION – Our first reading today (Is. 66, 18-21) comes from the time when the Jews were recovering from their long exile and enslavement in Babylon. It was a difficult time. Their cities, homes, and farms had lain in ruins for 50 years. The prophet who speaks is not a pessimist though. He sees great things for Jerusalem. He tells God's discouraged people some day people from all nations would come to worship the same God they worshipped. Even the Jewish priesthood would be opened up to foreigners. There are two lessons here for us: 1) spiritually the Jews are our ancestors and 2) God wants all people to be saved. The gate of heaven is open to everyone, a wonderful image. But Jesus, who always wishes to keep us in touch with reality, reminds us that, sadly, not everyone is headed that way (Lk 13, 22-30).

HOMILY – Jesus is asked a question we would all like to know the answer to. "Will only a few people be saved?" From the gospel, it sounds as if there are going to be lots of people in heaven, people coming from north and south, east and west. However, we would have liked a few more details, numbers, percentages perhaps, but I guess Jesus figures we can answer the question for ourselves by seeing how people live according to his teachings. If we live by his teachings, we're on our way to eternal happiness; if not, we'll lose out. After all he told us, "I am the way, the truth and the life."

When I was growing up, I think most people believed that it would be very hard to be saved. We worried about the smallest things such as whether we ate a little meat on Friday or drank anything before Communion. Society today has gone to the other extreme. People in today's society seem to think salvation is practically a given, that the only people not in heaven are those who had to work hard at avoiding getting there. Surveys today show almost 75% of Catholics say they can be good Catholics without attending church every Sunday. Half believe they can be a good Catholic without donating time or money to help the poor. It's like saying we can love God while choosing to ignore the important ways in which he asks us to serve him.

Heaven will have room for people from all nations, but there is still the "narrow gate" we have to pass through. In other words we can't take salvation for granted. The gospels were written in Greek and when Jesus said, "strive to enter through the narrow gate," the verb translated as "strive" in the original Greek is "agonízomai." We can hear the English word "agony" in this. "Agonízomai" means a lot more than "strive." It is a word often used in connection with the effort needed to win something – as to win in an Olympic event, or a performance, or a lawsuit or a contest. A good example would be a football game where the players work hard to get into condition and then they put everything they have into playing a good game. Can you see a coach saying to his players: "now get out there and strive to win today, guys?" Jesus is saying, "put everything you have into getting through that narrow gate." The image of "giving it all we have to win" is repeated in the next sentence when Jesus says, "many will attempt to enter but will not be strong enough."

It's not that we are competing with other people, like people do in sports, where if one person wins, others have to lose. What we have to compete with is our own selves, our own laziness, our own pride, our own self-centeredness, our own love of comfort or pleasure or material possessions; not to mention having to compete with the sinful attractions of society or the temptations of the devil. Life is a battleground and our Lord wants us to know it so we avoid the pitfalls, especially the pitfall of not realizing the importance of taking our faith seriously.

The image of the closed door that Jesus used in the gospel was a warning to the Jews not to take their position as "chosen people" for granted. It's a similar warning for all of us and the "closed door" reminds all of us that time will run out. Life is just so long and none of us know how long it will last.

All of this is very serious. Jesus doesn't tell us this to depress us or to discourage us or to scare us. He tells us this because he loves us. He wants us to be happy with him forever. All we need to do is look at the crucifix to know about his love. We celebrate that love today as we celebrate the Eucharist and it is that which gives us hope and joy.

22nd Sunday in Ordinary Time
September 2, 2007

HOMILY – (Sir 3:17-18, 20, 28-29; Heb 12:18-19, 22-24a; Luke 14:1, 7-14) A man about my age tells the story that recently he was on an airplane when an attractive lady, somewhere in her 20's, asked if she could sit next to him. His male ego soared. Soon they were chatting pleasantly. She told him it was her first airplane ride and a friend told her she would be less nervous if she sat next to someone she thought she could trust. She continued, saying: "You look just like my father."

A man died and when he got to heaven he made an appointment to meet with God. He said he had some questions that had puzzled him all his life that he had to have answered. So God met with him and he asked God: "Why did you make women with such beautiful faces?" God said: "So you would love them." Then he asked, "why did you give women such beautiful bodies?" Again God said "So you would love them." Then he asked: "Well, God, why did you make women - you know - not very smart?" God said: "So they would love you!"

Jesus said, "everyone who exalts himself will be humbled, but the one who humbles himself will be exalted." We all enjoy and even laugh at seeing someone who is full of themselves be cut down to size. I love the comment Golda Meir, the Prime Minister of Israel, made to a visiting diplomat who was trying to be very humble as he spoke to her. She brought him back down to earth with the comment: "Don't be so humble – you're not that great." I am certain Jesus had a great sense of humor and there was some humor in his little story about the person who tried to get into the most honored position at the dinner and he was asked to move down.

Jesus' teaching about taking the lowest place at a banquet with the hope that the host would say "My friend, move to a higher position," is not really an example of true humility. It only shows that even in everyday activities not being prideful can have an advantage. The person who picks the lowest place with the hope of being given more honors may not be any less proud than the person who pushes himself to the front of the line, but may simply be more clever. When I was younger I used to sit in the back of church and very proudly considered myself to be more humble than the rest of the people there. When I realized that where I was sitting had nothing to do with humility, I decided to sit up further and was amazed to find out how much more I got out of the Mass. To return to the gospel, for the Jews at the time of Jesus it was a very important thing as to where a person sat in an assembly or at a table. We are not quite so conscious about that today, but probably no more humble than the people of Jesus' day. We have created our own symbols of status in modern day society.

Jesus' teaching on true humility comes when he tells us about inviting the poor, the crippled, the lame and the blind; those who cannot repay the favor. Humility is the ability to see everyone as having been created in the image and likeness of God. Christ-like humility is a love for all people because they are loved by God. Jesus not only taught it but practiced it. He responded to all people. He often got in trouble with the religious leaders for associating too often with those who were considered to be on the bottom rung of the social ladder. I wonder if humility is not so much about what we think of ourselves, as it's about what we think of others and how we treat them. Of course, that includes what we think about God and how much we are aware of how dependent we are on our Creator.

The word "humility" comes from the Latin word humus, which means earth. No matter how wonderful we believe we may be, and each of us is a wonderful gift of God, we can't forget where we all came from. We can't forget that the Son of God came down to us to share his life with us. "I came that they might have life and may have it to the full." This will be a revelation of great wonder and we will discover how truly wonderful we are with God's grace.

As you come to Mass today, you are showing you recognize that dependence. Thus you are truly humble and are grounded in truth as you express it in our liturgy.

23rd Sunday in Ordinary Time
September 9, 2007

INTRODUCTION – (Wis 9:13-18b; Philemon: 9-10,12-17; Luke 14:25-33) When we think of slavery we think of the brutal situation of African slaves as it existed in our own country up until the middle of the 19th century. In the Roman Empire 20 centuries ago, where slavery was common, it was much different. Slaves came from nations and peoples that Rome had conquered. There were probably more white slaves than blacks. Many would have been educated or highly skilled and would have worked as musicians, scribes, craftsmen, teachers and even doctors. Slaves could be set free by their masters for good service or a slave could sometimes save up enough money to buy his or her own freedom. Today's second reading is about a slave, Onesimus. He escaped from his master, Philemon. By law Onesimus could have been put to death for escaping. He knew Paul for Paul had converted his master, Philemon to Christ. So, in fear for his life he ran to St. Paul, who was in prison at the time, probably in Ephesus. In those days prisoners were just locked up and they were not given three square meals a day or gymnasiums to work out in or cable TV's to entertain them. Unless a prisoner had someone to bring them food and take care of their needs, they probably would have starved to death. So, while Onesimus was with Paul, he took care of him and in the process Paul converted him to Christ. Paul thus sees himself as his spiritual father and refers to Onesimus as his own child. Paul felt an obligation to send him back to Philemon. He didn't feel right benefiting from a gift that had not been given to him. Paul asked Philemon in the letter we hear in today's second reading to receive Onesimus back, not as a piece of property, but as a brother in the Lord. Christianity transcends all other relationships as we hear in today's gospel.

HOMILY – Jesus was on his way to Jerusalem. St. Luke tells us he was traveling with great crowds. Jesus' disciples and the people following him were expecting some major changes in their lives when Jesus would arrive in Jerusalem. They expected Jesus would spearhead a resistance against their Roman oppressors, drive the Roman army out of Israel and take control of their land and their lives. For almost 600 years they lived under the rule of foreign kings. Now they would have their land back and their own king. Not only would they be free but life would be really wonderful for God's people for Jesus had unusual powers: he could heal the sick, feed the hungry, even raise the dead. No king in the history of the world would be so great! They anticipated Jesus would be their messiah and life would be fantastic. Jesus knew differently. He alone knew what was about to happen. So he told them, as he always spoke the truth, you can't follow me unless you hate your father and mother, wife and children, brothers and sisters and even your own life. You'll have a cross to pick up if you want to be my disciple. Like a man building a tower or a king going into battle, are they prepared for what they would face, are they sure they have what it takes?

One wonders what happened to the great crowds following him. Did they begin to drift off? There's one word in today's gospel that really shocks us (as I'm sure it shocked those who heard him): the word "hate." Certainly we know Jesus doesn't want us to hate anyone. So how could Jesus tell us to "hate" even those closest to us? The oldest document we have that reports Jesus' words is the Greek text of the gospels. Indeed, the Greek uses the verb "miseo" which means "hate." It is from that word that we get such English words as: misanthrope and misogyny. Miseo, however, has a secondary meaning which is "to prefer or favor something or someone less." And of course this is what Jesus means. St. Matthew helps us understand exactly what Jesus meant when he quoted Jesus in a parallel passage in his gospel, where Jesus said: "Whoever loves his father or mother, brother or sister, more than me is not worthy of me." The only thing Jesus wants us to truly hate is sin. But Jesus statement is still very challenging in that he is telling us if we are going to follow him, he must be more important to us than everyone and everything in our lives. He must be more important to us than even our own physical life. And indeed many Christians have had to face that dilemma and have given up life in this world in order to hold on to their faith. We call them martyrs, not the kind of martyrs who are suicide bombers who want to maim and kill, but martyrs in the sense of witnesses, witnesses to love: love for Jesus and love for others. In brief, we must be willing to lose everything rather than lose Jesus, or we are not his disciple.

Jesus would make a very poor politician. He doesn't tell us things we like to hear. He tells it like it is. He tells us it will not always be easy if we go with him. True, but I have seen over and over again, life is even harder if we try to live our lives without him. Only those who have made the decision to put Christ first know that they have really gained everything, for in Jesus is the fullness of life, the fullness of all that is good.

Too many Christians think of their faith like some kind of insurance. As long as they pay their premiums they're protected. And they try to figure out what is the minimum they can get by with to still be covered. For example, if the rule says go to Mass every Sunday, they figure well maybe once or twice a month will be just as good. If the rule says love your neighbor, well maybe I'll still be covered if I don't hurt anyone even if I never do anything to help anyone. I'm sure you can think of other examples of what one theologian called "cheap grace." The story of the tower half built is an image of our spiritual lives when they are built on half-hearted efforts. Heaven is not going to be "pie in the sky." Heaven is the happiness of surrendering ourselves to the greatest lover in the universe.

24th Sunday in Ordinary Time
September 16, 2007

INTRODUCTION – Our first reading (Exodus 32,7-11, 13-14) takes us back to the time of Moses, about 1300 years before Christ. The people of Israel were slaves who had just escaped from Egypt through God's power and Moses' leadership. God had just made them his people at Mt. Sinai through a covenant in which they pledged to honor Yahweh as their only God. God then called Moses to the top of Mt. Sinai to speak further with him. With their leader out of sight, the people got into trouble. Probably following the customs of the Egyptians, they tried to represent their God in animal form and they fashioned for themselves a golden calf. This is where our first reading begins. God is angry with his people. Notice, in speaking to Moses, he calls them "your people." Moses becomes an intercessor for the people and "convinces" God to be forgiving. His prayer displays total unselfishness. God, of course, forgives them. In the second reading we hear St. Paul describe what a sinful person he once was and how God was merciful to him (1 Tim, 1,12-17). Jesus gives us three beautiful parables on forgiveness in today's gospel (Lk. 15,1-32).

HOMILY – The criminal was being led to the courtroom by the bailiff. On the way the criminal asked if the judge was a tough one. The bailiff said "yes, he's as tough as Pontius Pilate." The criminal said "Was this Pilate judge tough? I ain't never heard of him since I ain't from this area."

Gratefully our Lord is not as tough on us as we were on him when he was accused before Pilate. Our readings today are about God's forgiveness. St. Paul tells us today

"You can depend on this as worthy of full acceptance: that Christ Jesus came into the world to save sinners."

We have just heard three parables about God's forgiveness. The first and second are very similar (about the good shepherd who seeks for the one lost sheep and the woman who seeks for the one lost coin). They tell us each and every one of us are important to God. God is not ready to say "I have so many people who believe in me and love me that this one or that one who doesn't isn't all that important." Each of us is important and is loved.

Then there is the story of the prodigal son. I think it is a magnificent description of the divine-human dynamic. Some people may find the story offensive and feel it is unfair as the elder son did. I often think, if God were to stick by what is fair and give all of us what we deserve, we would all be in trouble. I'm grateful for a God whose sense of love outweighs his sense of fairness. The story shows us that God's mercy is always there for us, but it depends on us as to whether we receive it. If we have moved away from God, God's mercy cannot reach us until we recognize where we are and "come to our senses" as the young man in today's gospel. The young man had to make a 180-degree turnaround. Notice he came home intending to be only a servant, a hired hand, but he was fully restored to his father's home and his father's love (less his inheritance which was already gone by this time).

I would like to mention another aspect of forgiveness between God and ourselves. Sometimes in life we have to forgive God. Terrible things happen in people's lives; that's part of being human. But sometimes people blame God for it and they spend many years angry at God because of what happened.

As with any anger or resentment, if we carry it around for long, it only eats us up inside. At times it may be understandable, but even then it does no good to hang on to it. It will only drag us down and destroy our peace of mind. The only thing any of us can do when we have questions about why things happen, or even when we get angry about things, is to reaffirm our faith that God is in charge and knows what he's doing. We have to trust that he loves us. Meditating on the cross can help us do that.

To sum all this up, we must be patient with God and trust him. Thankfully he is patient with us. If life takes us in the wrong direction, if we get lost, God will seek us out and take us back. But we have to choose not to stay lost and in humility head back home. The homecoming will be something to celebrate.

25th Sunday in Ordinary Time
September 23, 2007

INTRODUCTION – (Amos 8:4-7; 1 Tim 2:1-8; Luke 16:1-13) Our first reading comes from 2700 years ago. Israel was enjoying a time of great prosperity materially, but not spiritually. Their prosperity turned their minds away from God. They resented the Sabbath and the new moon. These were holy days on which work was forbidden. This kept them from what they considered the most important thing in life – making money. The ephah and shekel were weights they used to weigh the produce they bought and to weigh the produce they sold. Apparently they frequently used dishonest weights so they could cheat both supplier and customer. They even exploited their customers by mixing useless materials in with the products they wanted to sell – such as mixing chaff with the wheat. The world has changed in 2700 years, but human nature hasn't.

HOMILY – One time Mark Twain was involved in an argument about marriage with a Mormon. The Mormon said to Twain, "show me one place in the bible where having more than one wife is forbidden." Twain said, "that's easy. The bible said: 'no man can serve two masters.'"

Amos the prophet is not shy about telling God's people (us included) how God despises dishonesty and injustice. We just got a sampling of his preaching in today's first reading. In our gospel, we may be left a bit confused. It sounds as if Our Lord is speaking in a somewhat approving way of the dishonest steward. The steward may have squandered his master's property, enriched himself at his master's expense, or he may simply have been incompetent. Our Lord doesn't give us the details as to why he lost his job. Even if he was incompetent, he was bright enough to provide for his future. Before he left his position, he called in all the people who owed his master money and reduced the size of their debt. Then they would be indebted to him. Commentators suggest perhaps he was eliminating any commission that would have been due to him. Whatever was behind all of this, his dishonesty was not grand larceny or he would have been worried about jail rather than being worried about digging or begging. If we try to figure out the details, we'll miss the main point of the parable, and that's all a parable is – a simple story with one point. The point is people work very hard at providing for their wellbeing in this life. How hard or dedicated are we in providing for our spiritual wellbeing?

We are stewards of the time, the talents, and the material resources that we've been given. We can waste them, we can use them to serve only our own selfish interests, we can even use them to take advantage of others or to help others. We have to remember that we have One higher than ourselves to whom we will have to make an accounting of how well we've used the gifts we've been given.

Let me expand on this using two examples: time and money (two things that tell us where our priorities lie). How many times I've heard people say "I would like to pray more," "I would like to do more to help others, etc.," and "when I have more time." We all have the same amount of time, 24 hours. The secret of finding more time is good time management. The secret of good time management is setting priorities. In the past I frequently had difficulty getting all of my meditation in during the day. Once I decided to put meditation at the top of the list of things I had to do that day, I never had any difficulty after that. I'm not saying it's the very first thing I do in the morning, sometimes it's close to the last thing I do at night, but it always takes priority over any other discretionary time I have that day. Now I have to work on getting more exercise.

Another example involves money. Do we need it? Of course. It represents a roof over our heads and food on our tables. Too often we equate it with happiness and power but acquiring it can control people's lives. Jesus wants us to use it wisely but not let it become our master. One way of keeping things in perspective in this area is to tithe. I think that's what Our Lord means when he says, "make friends for yourselves with wicked money, so that when it fails, you will be welcomed into eternal dwellings."

Jesus tells us today as "children of the light" we have to provide for our spiritual lives just as seriously as people provide for their material needs. In other words, "be smart!" And we are being smart when we realize this life is only temporary (important as it may be), but the next life will last forever.

26th Sunday Ordinary Time
September 30, 2007

INTRODUCTION – (Amos 6:1a, 4-7; 1 Tim 6:11-16; Luke 16:19-31) Last week's first reading was from Amos and so is today's. Last week his prophecy was aimed at materialism and the oppression of the poor in the northern kingdom of Israel. Today's reading (Amos 6, 1a.4-7) seems directed to the people in the southern kingdom, "the complacent in Zion" (another name for Jerusalem). Perhaps this warning came after the Assyrians destroyed the northern kingdom which is called "Joseph" in today's reading. The complacent in Jerusalem were living pampered, comfortable lives, paying no attention to the devastation of the north and not concerned that their own country was headed toward the same fate because of their social and moral depravity. Amos was a true prophet whose words proved to be true.

HOMILY – Two men were in a private plane and they crashed on an island in the South Pacific. They both survived and one of the survivors right away surveyed the island and returned to his buddy to tell him they were doomed. The island was uninhabited and he could find no food or water. His buddy said "Not to worry. I make $250,000 a week." The man shook his friend and said "You don't understand. We're going to die. There's no one around, no food, no water." His buddy repeated: "Not to worry. I make $250,000 a week." Once more he screamed at him saying: "Don't you hear me. We're going to die. There's no food, no water, no one around." His buddy said: "Don't worry. I make $250,000 a week. I'm a Church going Christian and I tithe. My pastor will find us!"

Today's gospel (Lk. 16, 19-31) always leaves me

feeling guilty. I live a fairly comfortable life (I have a place to live, enough to eat, a bed to sleep in, I like to go out occasionally for a nice meal) and there are so many people like Lazarus out there. I try to give generously to charity, but the many people suffering all over the world is overwhelming. I'm sure many of you feel the same way. At the same time, I hate to be taken advantage of by phonies and that has happened more times than I would like to admit in the past 43 years. I just do what I can, knowing I can't solve every problem. It's good to be challenged by Jesus, however, because unless we're challenged, we easily become complacent and self centered. That's what happened to the people of Jerusalem at the time of Amos. That's what happened to the rich man in today's gospel.

Amos and Jesus are not saying a person will automatically be condemned because they are wealthy or will automatically be saved because they are poor. We will all be judged by the same law, the great commandment of love – love for God and love for others. I know people who are well off and at the same time they are very loving and generous, and I know people who are poor who are self-centered and egotistical. Having wealth is not necessarily a vice and being poor is not necessarily virtuous. The rich man in today's gospel was condemned not because he was a bad man, cruel, violent or evil; he was condemned for a lack of love. For him Lazarus just didn't exist. When the rich man wanted a favor from Lazarus in the next life, Abraham told him that there was a great chasm between the two of them. One commentator pointed out that the rich man was the one who created the chasm in the first place, holding Lazarus at arms length as if he wasn't there. Even in the next life, the rich man treated Lazarus as his lackey, not even addressing him but asking Abraham to send him to bring water or to go to warn his brothers.

Probably no society in the history of this world has enjoyed comfort than we do in America today. Kings and emperors did not live as well as most middle class families in America. Comfort is not sinful. But it is distracting and can be dangerous in that it can make us turn our attention increasingly toward ourselves and help us to forget about our responsibility to help others.

Our readings today force us to consider our personal attitude toward the material blessings we enjoy. The essence of today's readings is that no matter how hard we've worked or how talented we may be or how thrifty we've been, what we have is not just for our own self indulgence. We must share with others. The irony of this is that on the whole, those who have less of this world's goods are more generous than those who have been blessed with more. I say this because statistics show that, in general, the more income a person has the less, percentage wise, they give to charity. That is really ironic.

Most often Jesus' words are very comforting, but today's readings may make us uncomfortable, especially if we need to be made more sensitive to the suffering of others. If Jesus makes us uncomfortable it's to help us think about what God wants from us and if we are doing what he wants? Jesus wants only one thing, our salvation, and the only way that can happen is if we follow the way he has shown us.

If we keep remembering where our blessings come from, then we will be more likely to remember that they have not been given to us just to help us become selfish, self-centered people. Our great prayer of thanksgiving each week, which we call the Mass or the Eucharist, helps us to keep remembering where all our blessings come from.

27th Sunday in Ordinary Time
October 7, 2007

INTRODUCTION – (Habakkuk 1:2-3, 2:2-4; Lk 17:5-10) Six hundred years before Christ the Babylonians were the dominant power in the middle east. With their capital in modern day Iraq, their power stretched for hundreds of miles around. The prophet Habakkuk who speaks to us in today's first reading lived during the difficult 10 year period that began with the Babylonian army's first invasion into Judah but before they completely destroyed it. He asks God why God doesn't do something about the terrible things that were happening. God assures him things will be OK if the people just put their trust in God. Unfortunately they didn't, history tells us.

HOMILY – You may have heard about a book that came out recently entitled: Mother Teresa, Come Be My Light. It describes the uncertainty and discouragement Mother Teresa felt through most of her life. It was a surprise to many that such a holy person suffered such spiritual distress. Some have even suggested that maybe she didn't have a very strong faith if she encountered such difficulties in her spiritual life. That's because those who thought this way do not really understand faith.

The fact is that she had to have tremendous faith to be able to keep doing what she was doing, serving God, praying daily for two hours in church and not letting her uncertainty and discouragement cause her to give up or lose heart.

So many people assume that the saints lived ecstatically happy lives, that they were always in union with God and that they were never troubled by the trials and difficulties of life. Surely some of them had moments of ecstasy and some of them may have had lengthy periods of supreme joy in experiencing God's presence, but from what I've read of the saints, uncertainty and discouragement was normal. Some of them had long periods of uncertainty and discouragement such as John of the Cross, St. Teresa of Avila and St. Therese of Lisieux. Apparently for Mother Teresa, uncertainty and discouragement was a way of life. I cannot second guess the way God deals with those he loves, and surely God was giving Mother Teresa the opportunity to grow stronger in her faith, but looking at this from a natural point of view and considering the kind of ministry she was doing, ministering to the poorest of the poor and dying, it's not a great surprise she would encounter a lot of discouragement.

St. Teresa of Avila, who, as I remember spent almost 20 years without feeling God's presence, describes it as the "most painful life that can be imagined." She is often quoted as saying to God: "If this is the way you treat your friends, it's no wonder you have so few of them."

Faith means believing something as true without tangible evidence. If we always perceived God's love, we wouldn't need to have faith. We would know experientially that God loves us. But because we do not perceive it always, faith is necessary. There are moments when we feel God's presence, when we know his love, but most of us, most of the time, live our lives through faith. And when uncertainty or discouragement comes along, unfortunately many people crumble. The song is true for most of us: We walk by faith, not by sight.

What I'm talking about is what Spiritual writers refer to as spiritual darkness. It is also referred to as a desert experience when spiritual comfort and consolation is no where around. Spiritual writers tell us this desert experience, this spiritual dryness is part of everyone's faith journey. That is why we are encouraged to be constant in our prayers, whether we feel like it or not, whether they give us comfort or not. It is a time of growth. It is the only way to know the God who cannot be known through our own human resources.

Basically this is what Jesus tells us in today's gospel, in response to the apostles request "Increase our faith." Do what we have been commanded and consider ourselves as "unworthy of any praise." This is faith and this is how to increase it, praying and doing God's work not to get paid off with nice feelings, not to do it not to please ourselves (although there is some pleasure in knowing we are doing right) but we do what's right in order to please God. The payoff will come and it will be beyond our fondest dreams, but as the prophet Habakkuk tells us in the first reading: wait for it. It will not disappoint if we do not get discouraged and give up for the just one, because of his faith, shall live.

28th Sunday in Ordinary Time
October 14, 2007

INTRODUCTION – (2 Kgs 5:14-17; 2 Tim 2:8-13; Luke 17:11-19) Israel and Syria have been fighting with each other for centuries. Today's first reading takes us back to 850 BC when Syria was then called Aram. There was conflict then. Our reading is about an Aramean army general named Naaman. He had the dreaded disease of leprosy. His wife had a slave girl, an Israelite, who most probably was captured in battle. She told her master, Naaman, about a prophet in Israel who would be able to cure his disease. That prophet was Elisha. It must have taken a lot of humility and faith for this proud Aramean general to go into the territory of their enemy looking for Elisha. And when he located him, Elisha wouldn't even meet Naaman. He just told him through a messenger to go and bathe in the Jordan River. Naaman was insulted and decided to go back home. But his friends persuaded him to do as the prophet said. Thus our first reading begins. The reading prepares us for the gospel when we hear about Jesus healing 10 people who had leprosy. (I made some comments at 40 hours closing. They are printed below.)

FORTY HOURS – It's been years that I've preached at the closing of our Solemn Annual Eucharistic Devotions. I usually try to find another preacher, because most people hear me every week. But for special reasons I wanted to preach today.

Today we are celebrating four important anniversaries in our parish. Ted Schmidt, our deacon had been ordained 25 years. Unfortunately Ted couldn't be with us. He broke his hip and is still in the hospital, doing well, but not yet able to climb steps. Ted and Roselyn joined St. Boniface about the same time that I arrived here and I would have been lost without their very capable and dedicated ministry.

Sister Ann is our school principal and has been a wonderful gift to St. Boniface. She is celebrating 50 years in the Sisters of Mercy. She always tells people we hired her because she needed a job and couldn't find one. I find that hard to believe. I know when we were searching for a principal, Sr. Ann had just left St. Margaret of York and I called one of my friends who taught there, Sister Madonna, and asked her to tell me what she could about Sister Ann. By the time she finished I had already made up my mind to hire her, sight unseen. I've thanked God for her ever since. She will have a few things to say for herself when I finish.

Then there is Carol Ann Roosa. Carol has been

here ten years, but I have been working with Carol almost thirty. She first started out as our cleaning lady when I was at St. Columban. She eventually moved into the position of secretary. Since she has been here she has been and still is Pastoral Administrator, Director of Religious Education and Business Manager. She has been a great support in ministry and a good friend. She will be 60 tomorrow. She too will say a few words.

Then there is the fact that I turn 70 years old today. It is because today happens to be the day, I started thinking about the possibility of making this a day for a grand celebration with friends and including others who are celebrating significant life events in on it. There's not much I need to say about myself. Most of you know me pretty well by now.

Today we are having Evening Prayer, an ancient tradition of praise of God that goes back way before the time of Christ. It is a custom that has continued on in the Church until the present. Priests, deacons and religious are committed to daily prayer and Evening Prayer is part of our prayers. It's seldom celebrated with such solemnity as we see this evening except in the monasteries, but it is still part of our daily prayer.

It is a fitting way to conclude our Solemn Annual Eucharistic Devotions. Our prayer in the presence of the Blessed Sacrament remind us of the great gift of Jesus present with us in the Eucharist. St. John tells us that when Jesus spoke about giving us his body and blood to be our food and our drink, many of his followers walked away, thinking he was talking nonsense. He didn't stop them or try to explain away what he was telling them. He knew it was hard to understand, that's why he asked for faith. It's still hard to understand for many people, even us Christians.

As I turn 70, I was thinking of what it might have been like when I was an infant. One of the things an infant has to do is trust. When the father or mother feeds the child, the child trustfully (although instinctively) eats what they are given – most of the time. Sometimes a child eats what they are not given too. I was thinking of this in relation to the Eucharist. We are children of God. We don't have all the answers yet. So trustfully we eat and drink what God said will nourish us, food that will give us eternal life. "The bread that I will give is my flesh for the life of the world," Jesus told us.

We are grateful for this gift. We celebrate it each time we come to Mass. And we thank God for it at such special times as Holy Hours and Eucharistic Devotions. I don't think I would have survived emotionally or spiritually without the 20 minutes I spend each day in church.

[Sister Ann and Carol Roosa will now speak, then I'll wrap it up.]

We are celebrating now in prayer and praise. Shortly we will go over to the cafeteria of school to continue celebrating God's many blessings. I have asked Sister Ann and Carol to speak now so we won't have any speeches during supper time. I just want everyone to enjoy the evening and the meal, uninterrupted. You will have to look around for the food. There are tables with food along three walls of the cafeteria and the drinks are in the hall. And please notice the pictures at the end of the hall. I do want to end with a special thank you to Ruthann Sammarco who, along with help from several others, coordinated the dinner, a special thank you to Deacon Jerry Yetter who is the server at our liturgy tonight and, who with Mary Ellen his wife helps me in so many other ways and a special thank you to

Don Auberger and the choir for their inspiring ministry of song. And I want to thank my priest friends for coming and all of you for coming.

29th Sunday in Ordinary Time
October 21, 2007

INTRODUCTION – (Exod 17:8-13; 2 Tim 3:14-4:2; Luke 18:1-8) As Moses led God's people from Egypt, through the desert, to the Promised Land, they encountered numerous threats to their safety such as the army of Pharaoh, the Reed Sea they had to cross, the lack of water and food in the desert. One of the difficulties they had to face was opposition from those peoples whose lands they had to pass through. Today's reading speaks of an attack by Amalek, a desert tribe living south of the Dead Sea. Moses positioned himself on a nearby hill, holding his arms high in prayer with the staff of God in his hands. This is the same staff by which Moses worked such wonders in Egypt. His powerful prayer directly affected the outcome of the battle and his persistence in prayer resulted in victory. It is a good model of how Jesus tells us we should pray in today's gospel.

HOMILY – When I was growing up, children were forbidden for us to keep pestering our parents for something. When my mother or father said "no," especially my father, that was the end of any discussion. Jesus tells us with God the opposite is true. God doesn't mind being pestered; on the contrary, he prefers it. In the male dominated society of Jesus' day, widows had no significant social standing. It would not have been unusual for widows to be taken advantage of and for them to have little recourse. This widow's only recourse to justice was to pester the judge until he got tired of hearing from her. And so she did. Would she have struck him, literally given him a black eye? Would she have hurt him by destroying his reputation? Or would she have just driven him crazy? There are various ways of interpreting the Greek verb here. The main point is clear. She was relentless in seeking a just settlement for herself. That's how we should pray.

Why does our Lord tell us to pray in that way? He, who knows how many hairs are on the top of our head, knows what we need. He hears every word we say, every thought we have, and he knows everything we need. He doesn't need reminders. He is infinite. He's not like the unjust judge who had little or no regard for the widow. He loves each of us more than we can begin to imagine. Meditate on the cross for proof of that. And he's not too busy. My dad would seldom pray for himself. He always said God has too many important things to worry about. He can't be worried about me. It sounds like an expression of humility, but in reality it is saying God is not infinite. That God is limited like we are and he can't handle everything he has to do. All these ideas add to the mystery of why he tells us to keep asking.

One can only speculate why God wants us to pester him. Maybe it's his way of getting to hear from some of us sometimes. Maybe it's his way of not letting us forget he is our Father and we depend totally on him. Maybe it's his way of trying to get us to enter into more of a relationship with him. Maybe it's his way of helping us know that what we ask for is truly what we want. Maybe it's his way of teaching us how to listen or how to solve our own problems. Maybe what we are praying for is too big of a request to happen quickly such as if we pray for the end of abortion or war. Too many hearts have to be changed before it happens and lots more prayers are needed before it can take place. Maybe prayer itself is a kind of spiritual power or energy that can affect what we are asking for. Just as a tiny seed has in it the energy of life and by planting seed life is released, so maybe when we pray, love or energy moves out of us and focuses itself like a laser on the person or event we are praying for. I suppose we could speculate all day, but one thing is clear, Jesus said don't quit praying.

Prayer is an act of faith in God and in God's love. Part of the reason people give up praying too soon is because they don't believe strongly enough. That's why I think Jesus said at the end of the gospel: "When the Son of Man comes, will he find faith on earth?" Part of the reason people give up is because we are too spoiled. If our refrigerator is broken, we get a new one. If we want to watch a certain program on TV, we just press a button. If we're hungry, we just pop an already prepared dinner in the microwave. If we want to hear good music, we turn on WGUC or turn on a CD. We blame God for not answering our prayers fast enough, but perhaps the problem is ours. We lack patience; we expect God to jump when we say jump.

I've thought of my own prayers. I ask for everything from being able to find a parking place when I'm in a hurry to good health to world peace. I pray for the safety of my friends and I pray for blessings on my parish and for the sick. I ask for help in the work I do. But I don't spend a lot of time asking for specific things. When I pray, it's a whole variety of things that go through my mind. I question God and wonder why God does what God does. I wonder what God is like. I reflect on Scripture. I thank God often and sometimes I just sit quietly with God. As long as we don't quit praying, our prayer and our relationship with God will deepen. I know it will, and now we continue on praying the greatest prayer of all, the Mass. Amen.

30th Sunday in Ordinary Time
October 28, 2007

HOMILY – (Sir 35:12-14, 16-18; 2 Tim 4:6-8, 16-18; Luke 18:9-14) A very stern and humorless lady was not feeling well and made an appointment to see a doctor. The doctor began by asking his new patient some basic questions. "Do you drink at all?" "I never touch alcohol!" She said with great distain. "Do you smoke?" "I never go near tobacco!" She was insulted by the question. "What about your sleeping habits?" "I go to bed early every night," she said haughtily. "I have no time for late-night partying and carousing. I am a busy woman. I am in bed by ten and up by six every morning." "I see," said the doctor, making notes on the chart. "Now exactly what's been the problem?" "I have been having terrible headaches," she said. "I think I see your problem," the doctor said. "your halo is too tight."

I wonder if the Pharisee in today's gospel had problems with headaches. Those who heard Jesus would have understood the parable up until the last line. Jesus description of the Pharisee was accurate as well as his description of the tax collector. It was that last line that would have blown their minds: "The tax collector went home justified, the other did not." Pharisees were holy people. Their main desire in life was to live by God's law as perfectly as possible. It is certainly an admirable goal to follow God's law faithfully. Tax collectors were despised as among the worst of sinners. They were seen as traitors in that they collected taxes for the hated Romans who controlled the Holy Land in Jesus' day.

More than that, they made their living on the taxes they collected and most likely they were not as honest as they should have been. As long as they gave the Roman Governor what was due, anything extra they managed to collect or extort was theirs. Some of them grew quite wealthy. In his parable Jesus was not trying to put down people who try to be good and applaud people who aren't. The parable is really all about prayer. Do you remember last week's gospel when Jesus told the story of the unjust judge and the poor widow who badgered him until she got a just settlement. It was a lesson in perseverance in prayer. Today he gives us another lesson in prayer.

At first it sounds as if the prayer of the Pharisee is a good prayer. It starts off with: "O God, I thank you..." Not a bad start. Thanking God should always be part of everyone's prayer. If we can honestly say we've been pretty decent people, that's a good thing to thank God for. I often thank God for the parents I had, the education I had and the faith I have. I would hate to think where I would have ended up without the values I've been taught and the opportunities and grace God has given me. But if we examine the so called prayer of the Pharisee, we will see it is no prayer at all. Jesus tells us the Pharisee spoke this prayer to himself. He wasn't talking to God but to himself. His prayer was filled with self-pride (not giving God the credit for his virtuous life) and with contempt of others who were not as good as he thought he was. If he had really given God thanks for the help and grace he had received that aided him to become the good person he was, if he had said a prayer for the tax-collector who may not have received the same opportunities and blessings in life that the Pharisee had received, then that would have been a real prayer. But that's not the way it was. The tax-collector is the one who really prayed an honest prayer. He really connected with God in recognizing his own sinfulness and asking forgiveness. In honestly connecting with God he was justified; i.e., he was forgiven.

We only find this parable in St. Luke's gospel, which is sometimes referred to as the gospel of prayer. It tells us our prayer must be genuine, it must be honest, it must be humble. If the Pharisee wasn't such a pompous guy he probably would have been a pretty nice person. I'll bet his wife found him to be a royal pain. It's hard to live with someone who is perfect. I've tried to do marriage counseling with people like that. I wasn't very successful. Someone who thinks they are perfect is not only blind to their own faults, they are quite conscious of the faults of others and feel it is their duty to constantly point them out.

I could talk a long time about pride and humility, honesty and dishonesty, being judgmental, looking down on others, etc. but I won't. That would take another 45 minutes. We might just take a moment and ask ourselves "how do I pray?" To pray well we do not have to think of ourselves as no good, we do not have to sit in the back of church, we do not have to put ourselves down. We do have to be honest and humble, and if we've sinned, ask for forgiveness. Also at least once a week, if not more often, we need to spend some time recognizing how we've been blessed and saying "thanks" for all we've been given. We do that most perfectly in the Eucharist which we now celebrate. Amen

All Saints
November 1, 2007

INTRODUCTION – (Rev 7:2-4,9-14; 1 John 3:1-3; Matt 5:1-12a) Our first reading is from the book of Revelation. The section just preceding today's passage described the end of the world. The sun became dark and the moon became red as blood and there was a great earthquake all over the earth. People tried to hide from all these terrible things and they asked: "Who can survive?" Today's reading answers the question – those who have followed Christ faithfully. The number 144,000 is a symbolic number, symbolizing perfection. Notice after it refers to the 144,000 it speaks of those who are saved as such a large crowd that no one could count them.

HOMILY – It's hard to believe it's already November. As this year comes to an end we are reminded that time in this life will come to an end for each one of us. It's not something most of us enjoy thinking about, but the Church reminds us through various liturgies at this time of the year that this life is not all there is. God has greater things prepared for us. And so we begin the month with the feast of All Saints, giving us an image of the glory God intends for us if we just travel along the way he has pointed out for us.

The first reading today is from the last book of the bible giving us a lot of hope that we will be among those who will enjoy God's love for all eternity. Even though Jesus told us that those who take the easy way that leads to destruction are many, and there are few who enter into life through the narrow gate, those few are still quite a sizeable number, a number too large to count. Those who have been designated by the Church as saints are very easy to count. It's obvious that the great number of saints our first reading tells us about include ordinary people like us, or like neighbors we've known, or parents or grandparents or relatives we've loved.

The hope that our first reading gives us is underscored in our second reading where we hear that "we are God's children." This is not just a nice, feel-good, poetic term, it is in fact what we really are if we have God's grace in us.

Our gospel reading shows us Jesus preaching the beatitudes as he begins the Sermon on the Mount. As we hear the beatitudes, we can perhaps think of some of the great saints who lived out the various beatitudes. For example: "blessed are the single hearted" such as Mother Teresa, or "blessed are the poor in spirit" like St. Francis of Assisi, or "blessed are those persecuted for holiness sake" such as St. Lawrence or St. Boniface. Which of the beatitudes do you think appeals most to you? On this day of All Saints it might be a good idea to choose one of the beatitudes and try to live it out more fully. I believe if we do, we will find that we are at the same time living out all the others to a greater degree as well. " Let us remember that Jesus ends them with these words: "Be glad and rejoice, for your reward will be great in heaven."

31st Sunday in Ordinary Time
November 4, 2007

INTRODUCTION – (Wis 11:22-12:2; 2 Thess 1:11-2:2; Luke 19:1-10) Our first reading begins with the line: "Before the Lord, the whole universe is as a grain from a balance or a drop of morning dew." The balance the author is speaking of is a balancing scale where a grain would be a tiny weight that weighed something like gold or silver. The author could have had no idea how vast the universe is, but he is true in telling us God is greater. After this statement, the author of our reading goes into a long prayer of praise of God's greatness and love.

HOMILY – To help you see the humor and the drama in today's gospel, I would like you to imagine that the pope is making a visit to Washington D.C. Most of Washington's politicians and lawyers, lobbyists and ordinary people show up to welcome him. Dick Cheney, our vice president who also wanted to see the pope, was out hunting and he showed up late. The crowd was too big for him to get through and, since he is a little shorter than average, he wasn't able to see over the heads of people in the crowd. To see the pope's motorcade, Dick Cheney climbs up one of the cherry trees so he can see better. A few in the crowd may have enjoyed watching Dick Cheney climb a tree. But then the pope saw him there and said "Dick, hurry and get down. I'm going to stay with you this evening." Watching him "hurry down" might have drawn a few more chuckles. The pope might have even laughed, but then things got less funny. People started grumbling. The pope is playing partisan politics. The pope should be concerned about the poor and here he is catering to the rich. Then there would be those who believe that Dick Cheney is not a totally honest and virtuous person and they wonder why the pope is hanging out with people like that. Right away Dick Cheney declares that he's giving half of his oil stock to Catholic Charities and he is going to make right any mistakes that he was responsible for in the Bush administration!

Now you have a feel for the humor and the drama that one might have felt on that particular day when Jesus passed through Jericho. I want to clarify one thing: I used Dick Cheney as an example only because he is well known and because he probably wouldn't look very dignified climbing up or down a cherry tree. Zaccheus would have been well known. He was the chief tax collector in the area whose wealth most likely came from gouging the poor people he collected taxes from. The people would have viewed him as a traitor and a first rate crook. So lets reflect on what happened when Jesus asked Zaccheus to hurry down from the tree. Jesus had already seen the potential goodness in this man. With just a simple word from Jesus, new life filled Zaccheus. Jesus asked only for a meal and a place to stay for the night, but the heart of Zaccheus opened up completely. He announced he would make amends if he had defrauded anyone (as he surely had, for fourfold restitution was traditional in cases of flagrant theft). Furthermore, he committed himself to giving half of his money to the poor. The gospels never tell us of Jesus smiling, but surely on this occasion he must have been grinning from ear to ear.

The first reading tells us in prayer: God, "you love all things that are and loathe nothing that you have made." Although God's love was there before Zaccheus was even born, Zaccheus had to do something to open himself to that love. And he did. He climbed a tree and before he knew it, Jesus was a guest in his home. Not only was Jesus his guest, but something else wonderful happened to Zaccheus. Zaccheus discovered that genuine happiness was not in material wealth but in God's love and in loving others. The gospel describes Zaccheus as small, but his encounter with Jesus allowed him to grow – not in stature but in maturity and love and joy.

What is the tree that we have to climb to see Jesus? In what way do we have to go out of our way to allow God to take possession of us? Do we need to spend more time in prayer? Do we need to be more generous with our money? Do we need to rise above our fears and mistrust and allow God to have more control in our lives? Do we need to come to Mass more often, perhaps even when we are not obligated to come? Do we need to forgive or to be forgiven? Do we need to control our impatience and trust more? The tree that we need to climb in order to see Jesus better may take many forms. Do we want to see Jesus badly enough to climb it?

No matter how small we may think we are, no matter how bad we may have been, no matter how insignificant we may feel, God loves us and he offers us his friendship and his life — forever. Today at Mass he is inviting himself into our lives. As Jesus states in the Book of Revelation: "Behold I stand at the door and knock." How far will we open the door of our hearts to let him in?

32nd Sunday in Ordinary Time
November 11, 2007

INTRODUCTION – (2 Macc 7:1-2, 9-14; 2 Thess 2:16-3:5; Luke 20:27-38) Alexander the Great built an empire that stretched from Sicily and Egypt all the way to India. This included Israel. About a hundred and fifty years after Alexander died, the Greeks still governed the area. By that time they started enforcing Greek culture and religion on all those whom they ruled. In Israel this meant, for example, that it was a crime to circumcise a child. Copies of the Scriptures were burned. Jews could not follow their dietary laws or celebrate their usual feasts. The worship of Greek gods and goddesses was required. Some of the Jews gave in to the Greeks, others fought hard to hold on to their traditional faith in Yahweh. Our first reading gives us just a hint of how terrible this time was for the Jews. This reading is chosen because it reflects their faith in the resurrection of those who are faithful to Yahweh, and it prepares us for the gospel which also deals with the topic of resurrection.

HOMILY – St. Paul said clearly, "If Christ is not risen, vain is our preaching and vain is your faith." Paul's words remind us how essential to our faith is the resurrection. It is the death and resurrection of Christ we celebrate each week at the Eucharist. We recall this mystery in the spring at Easter time because that's when Jesus died and rose. At this time of the year we reflect on death and resurrection because the year is coming to an end. The Church reminds us our own lives will also come to an end some day. We have been called to share in Christ's risen life at the end of time. Most of us do not like to think about this life coming to an end, but if we don't think about it, we will not be very well prepared for it. It is important that we be prepared, because it's only by being prepared through our faithfulness to Christ that we will enjoy the wonderful things that are ahead for us. Jesus said: "I came that they may have life and have it more abundantly." That more abundant life will be with him forever in risen glory.

Our first reading describes the heroic faith of many Jews during the difficult period when the Greeks were attempting to impose paganism on the Jewish people. That was about a century and a half before the birth of Christ. The faith that these faithful Jews showed was amazing, considering that the Jews had not had a long tradition of belief in the resurrection. That was a concept that only developed a few hundred years before Christ. We see from the gospel that not even all of the religious leaders of Jesus' day believed in the resurrection. The Sadducees were of the priestly class. We hear them in today's gospel asking Jesus a ridiculous question, not because they were interested in the answer, but because they wanted to embarrass him with a dilemma they thought he wouldn't be able to answer. Jesus answered them by saying their idea of the next life was incorrect. The law that Moses wrote about a man taking his brother's wife if his brother were to die was meant to preserve a deceased man's name and memory through offspring, to protect inheritance, and to secure the safety of the widow. There would be no need for all of that in the next life.

Jesus did not tell us much of what it will be like in the next life, because it will be so much different from anything we now know. It will not be a continuation of our present life. We will have our bodies back, not with all our aches and pains and imperfections, but in some glorified form. After our spirit enters into the glory of God's kingdom, we hope, then at the time of the resurrection, we will receive a body to match – a body that will radiate also God's glory. It is beyond our understanding now what this might be like. C.S. Lewis tried to describe it this way. He said a person who has experienced bodily resurrection "would have gone through as big a change as a [stone] statue...[being] changed from being a carved stone to being a real man."

The Lord reminds us today that the work of creation is not finished. Our spirits and the glorified body that we will have will be infused with the strength and beauty and glory and immortality of God. But we need to cooperate with this plan that God has for us. This is why Christ came to us, to show us the way. This is one of the reasons why we gather for the Eucharist each week - to remember what Jesus taught us and to remember what he did for us and why.

33rd Sunday in Ordinary Time
November 18, 2007

INTRODUCTION – (Mal 3:19-20a; 2 Thess 3:7-12; Luke 21:5-19) In our first reading today we hear from the prophet Malachi who lived about 470 years before Christ. Many Jews at that time were apathetic about their religious duties and about keeping the Commandments. He warns his listeners that the day of reward and punishment is coming. Fire is the symbol that represents both the reward and the punishment. It will be scorching heat for those who have not followed God's ways, and will bring warmth and healing to those who have been faithful.

HOMILY – I'm always feeling nervous around this time of the year. It's the season when they shoot turkeys!

In case you are wondering why the church is decorated in this fashion, we had our children's Mass on Friday and the theme was Thanksgiving. The tail feathers on the turkey on the altar each mention something that each kindergarten child is thankful for (their family, their teacher, their parents, their dog, their brother!) And the trees have fruit hanging on them, with lists of things the children in other grades are grateful for. As we all know, true gratitude not only inspires us to say "thank you" but also moves us to share our blessings. So the children brought in cans of food for our St. Vincent de Paul food pantry. By the way, about 85 to 90 percent of our school children come from families whose income is below the poverty line. One does not have to be rich to be generous and to share.

Life has its ups and downs. We have happy times and we have tragic times. And the Scripture readings this week remind us of both, the good times and bad. Today's gospel is about difficult times. It reminds us that some day this world, which we love, (most of the time) will come to an end. The destruction of the Temple was just a prelude to the end of all things that we treasure. We need to remember that this will happen, so we keep our priorities straight and make God's Kingdom our greatest treasure for that will never end.

On Thursday of this week, we think of the blessings we have received and we give thanks. We need to know, however, that gratitude is an attitude and not just something that takes place once a year. I've always preached that thankfulness is the key to joy. This is supported now by objective psychological research. Two psychologists from the University of Miami took three groups and randomly assigned them to take time once a week to focus on one of three things: hassles, things for which they were grateful, and ordinary things. The results were that people who focused on things for which they were grateful saw their lives in favorable terms. They had fewer headaches or colds, and they took better care of themselves . Their energy and joy and their willingness to help others was noticed by those who knew them. This did not happen with the other two groups. Further studies have confirmed those results. That's fantastic. If you want to live happier, healthier, more optimistic lives, practice being more grateful. Psychology is just confirming what we've always been taught. St. Paul, two millennia ago, said "Dedicate yourselves to thankfulness...Sing gratefully to God from your hearts in psalms, hymns and inspired songs. Whatever you do, whether in speech or in action, do it in the name of the Lord Jesus. Give thanks to God the Father through him." (Col. 3, 15-17) The Church tries to help us to become grateful if we're not, or to remain grateful if we are, by telling us to come to Mass every week. Another word for Mass is Eucharist, a Greek word meaning Thanksgiving. Too many people think Thanksgiving is all about lots of food and lots of football. That will not do the job for our spirits that real gratitude will do.

The biggest obstacle to a grateful spirit is our own negativism. We tend to dwell on our problems, on what we don't have, on what's wrong with our lives. Certainly we have to try to deal with problems when they arise, but some things we just have to live with. If we are always focused on problems, that's a path that leads to depression. To develop an attitude of gratitude, we have to consciously focus on what's right with our lives, what cheers us up, what we have, not what we wish we had. It takes a conscious effort and discipline to do this sometimes. When we begin seeing how blessed we are, it's like opening the shade and letting in the sunshine, or as Malachi says it, "there will arise the sun of justice with its healing rays."

Gratitude expressed to others almost always comes back around. One study, for example, showed that waitresses who wrote "thank you" on the check they presented at the end of a meal received on average 11% more tips than those who didn't. Gratitude does have a boomerang effect.

We are reminded in Mass today how blessed we are. Sure there will be difficult times in life, but God will not abandon us. He will help us through. If we follow the wisdom and the way of life he has revealed to us we can, with gratitude, look forward to eternal joy. "Not a hair on your head will be destroyed. By your perseverance you will secure your lives." Amen.

Christ the King
November 25, 2007

INTRODUCTION – (2 Sam 5:1-3; Col 1:12-20; Luke 23:35-43) When the first king of Israel, King Saul, was killed in battle, the southern part of Israel chose David as their king. The northern part chose Ishbaal, King Saul's son, to be their king. Ishbaal was inept and after seven years of chaos, the northern tribes turned to David and asked him to rule them also. This is where our first reading comes in. David was a successful leader and, in spite of some serious misbehavior, was viewed throughout Jewish history as an ideal king. The Jews always hoped for another king like him. When a king assumed his office, he was anointed and thus the ideal king the Jews longed for was often referred to as "the anointed one." The Hebrew word for this is "Mashiah," or as we say it: "Messiah." When Mashiah is translated into Greek we have "Χριστός." So when we call Jesus "Christ" we are in effect saying Jesus, the King. Christ's kingdom is not an earthly one, as St. Paul tells us, but it is eternal and a sharing in God's own authority and power.

HOMILY – This will be my last homily for this year. Before everyone cheers or wonders whether I am taking an extended vacation, I should tell you I'm talking about the liturgical year – otherwise known as the Church year. Next Sunday is the first Sunday of Advent, and we begin again a new Church year, preparing ourselves to celebrate Christ's birth. Before we know it, we're into Ash Wednesday, and it is especially early this year. The last time Lent came so early in the spring (and that's because Easter is early) was 89 years ago. Starting next Sunday, then, we begin to recall the major events of Jesus life: his birth, his death, resurrection, ascension and his sending of the Holy Spirit. After Pentecost, as usual, we hear about his miracles and his teaching as presented to us in St. Matthew's gospel. And as usual, at the end of the liturgical year, we will again celebrate the feast of Christ the King.

The feast of Christ the King was established in 1925 by Pope Pius XI. You might wonder, didn't Pius XI know kings are not so popular any more? But what else could we call Christ? Should we call him instead a president, a prime minister, the chairman of the board, a dictator, president for life? The title "King" is most fitting for Christ. But he is not the same as any other king. His power is absolute and eternal. He has received his authority and power from God the Father and that will never change.

When we think of kings, it is automatic to associate them with castles and crowns, royal robes, jewelry, servants, armies and various symbols of wealth and power. Today Jesus, our king, is pictured hanging on the cross, his crown a crown of thorns. His small group of followers is nowhere to be found except for his mother, one faithful Apostle, and a couple of women. No rings were on his fingers, just nails in his hands and feet. No royal robes, instead he was most likely stripped naked as was the Roman custom. Later centuries have covered him over with a loin cloth for modesty. No one is cheering him or praising him. His enemies are outdoing each other mocking him. After three years working to establish a kingdom of love, he is condemned as a criminal, tortured and executed. He warned his followers some of them would suffer in a similar fashion. It's a wonder he had any followers at all.

I am always impressed when I think of what Jesus did in three years. Moses labored for 40 years, Buddha 45 years, and Muhammad 23. The carpenter on the cross, with the sign above his head, Jesus Christ, king of the Jews, who came from a politically and religiously insignificant part of an insignificant country, influenced this world more than any human being that ever lived. After two thousand years a billion people, including ourselves, call him our king! If some of his followers reflected his teachings more faithfully, there might be six billion who now follow him. Jesus is a king who does not parade around in worldly glory or demonstrate worldly power. However, he is greater than any king who ever lived, for he is "the image of the invisible God, the firstborn of all creation."

Our king does not rule by arms and weapons. Arms and weapons get people's attention. Without having someone to stand over us with a club or a gun, we are tempted to feel "why do I have to do what they tell me?" A lot of people feel that about Jesus. The people who put him on a cross felt that way, except for his few friends and the thief who asked to be remembered when Jesus entered his kingdom. The Jewish leaders thought they would be rid of this troublemaker, this bossy person who went around telling people how they should live. They didn't understand the power that he lived by and taught by, the power of love. He will always be a king who rules with love, but whether or not he is king in our lives and in our hearts is up to us. If we respond to him in love, it will lead us into his kingdom of new life.

A cartoon in the New Yorker showed two fellows walking to lunch one day and the one was complaining to the other: "my boss keeps telling me what to do." Authority is not popular, we like to make our own rules, even with regard to God. The new age theology, which is really a return to paganism, views Christ as a nice guy who overlooks our bad behavior and is going to reward all of us in the end, no matter how we've lived. He will forgive us if we turn to him. Notice his words of forgiveness were directed only to one of the two crucified with him. We cannot take our salvation lightly. The cross was not a joy ride for Jesus. Salvation is serious business and Jesus suffered in order to win salvation for us. But he can only save us if we do not forget that he is always our king, not just in an abstract way but in our concrete, everyday lives. Amen.

A Priest Is a Gift from God

by Rita Ring

How to Become a
Shepherd of Christ Associate

The Shepherds of Christ has prayer chapters all over the world praying for the priests, the Church and the world. These prayers that Father Carter compiled in the summer of 1994 began this worldwide network of prayer. Currently the prayers are in eight languages with the Church's Imprimatur. Fr. Carter had the approval of his Jesuit provincial for this movement, writing the Newsletter every 2  months for 6 1/2 years. After his death, and with his direction, we in the Shepherds of Christ circulated the Priestly Newsletter Book II to 95,000 priests with other writings. We have prayed daily for the priests, the Church, and the world since 1994. Associates are called to join prayer Chapters and help us circulate this newsletter centered on spreading devotion to the Sacred Heart and Immaculate Heart and helping to renew the Church through greater holiness. Please form a Prayer Chapter & order a Prayer Manual.

Apostles of the Eucharistic Heart of Jesus

The Shepherds of Christ have people dedicated to spending two hours weekly before the Blessed Sacrament in the Tabernacle. They pray for the following intentions:

1) For the spread of the devotion to the Hearts of Jesus and Mary culminating in the reign of the Sacred Heart and the triumph of the Immaculate Heart.

2) For the Pope.

3) For all bishops of the world.

4) For all priests.

5) For all sisters and brothers in religious life.

6) For all members of the Shepherds of Christ Movement, and for the spread of this movement to the world.

7) For all members of the Catholic Church.

8) For all members of the human family.

9) For all souls in purgatory.

This movement, *Apostles of the Eucharistic Heart of Jesus*, was began with Fr. Carter. Please inquire. Shepherds of Christ Ministries P.O. Box 627, China, Indiana 47250 USA or 1-888-211-3041 or info@sofc.org

Prayer for Union with Jesus

Come to me, Lord, and possess my soul. Come into my heart and permeate my soul. Help me to sit in silence with You and let You work in my heart.

I am Yours to possess. I am Yours to use. I want to be selfless and only exist in You. Help me to spoon out all that is me and be an empty vessel ready to be filled by You. Help me to die to myself and live only for You. Use me as You will. Let me never draw my attention back to myself. I only want to operate as You do, dwelling within me.

I am Yours, Lord. I want to have my life in You. I want to do the will of the Father. Give me the strength to put aside the world and let You operate my very being. Help me to act as You desire. Strengthen me against the distractions of the devil to take me from Your work.

When I worry, I have taken my focus off of You and placed it on myself. Help me not to give in to the promptings of others to change what in my heart You are making very clear to me. I worship You, I adore You and I love You. Come and dwell in me now.

Prayer Before the
Holy Sacrifice of the Mass

Let me be a holy sacrifice and unite with God in the sacrament of His greatest love.

I want to be one in Him in this act of love, where He gives Himself to me and I give myself as a sacrifice to Him. Let me be a holy sacrifice as I become one with Him in this my act of greatest love to Him.

Let me unite with Him more, that I may more deeply love Him. May I help make reparation to His adorable Heart and the heart of His Mother, Mary. With greatest love, I offer myself to You and pray that You will accept my sacrifice of greatest love. I give myself to You and unite in Your gift of Yourself to me. Come and possess my soul.

Cleanse me, strengthen me, heal me. Dear Holy Spirit act in the heart of Mary to make me more and more like Jesus.

Father, I offer this my sacrifice, myself united to Jesus in the Holy Spirit to You. Help me to love God more deeply in this act of my greatest love.

Give me the grace to grow in my knowledge, love and service of You and for this to be my greatest participation in the Mass. Give me the greatest graces to love You so deeply in this Mass, You who are so worthy of my love.

Father Carter requested
that these be prayed in prayer
chapters all over the world.

Shepherds of Christ

Prayers

Shepherds of Christ Associates

PRAYER MANUAL

Shepherds of Christ Publications
China, Indiana

Imprimi Potest: Rev. Bradley M. Schaeffer, S.J.
  Provincial
  Chicago Province, The Society of Jesus

Imprimatur: Most Rev. Carl K. Moeddel
  Auxiliary Bishop
  Archdiocese of Cincinnati

The Shepherds of Christ Associates Prayer Manual is published by Shepherds of Christ Publications, an arm of Shepherds of Christ Ministries, P.O. Box 627 China, Indiana 47250 USA.

  Founder, Shepherds of Christ Ministries:
  Father Edward J. Carter, S.J.

  For more information contact:
  Shepherds of Christ Associates
  P.O. Box 627
  China, Indiana 47250- USA
  Tel. 812-273-8405
  Toll Free: 1-888-211-3041
  Fax 812-273-3182

Chapter Meeting
Prayer Format

The prayer format below should be followed at chapter meetings of *Shepherds of Christ Associates*. All prayers, not just those said specifically for priests, should include the intention of praying for all the needs of priests the world over.

1. **Hymns.** Hymns may be sung at any point of the prayer part of the meeting.

2. **Holy Spirit Prayer.** Come, Holy Spirit, almighty Sanctifier, God of love, who filled the Virgin Mary with grace, who wonderfully changed the hearts of the apostles, who endowed all Your martyrs with miraculous courage, come and sanctify us. Enlighten our minds, strengthen our wills, purify our consciences, rectify our judgment, set our hearts on fire, and preserve us from the misfortunes of resisting Your inspirations. Amen.

3. **The Rosary.**

4. **Salve Regina.** "Hail Holy Queen, Mother of mercy, our life, our sweetness, and our hope. To you do we cry, poor banished children of Eve. To you do we send up our sighs, our mourning, our weeping in this vale of tears. Turn, then, most gracious advocate, your eyes of mercy toward us and after this, our exile, show unto us the blessed fruit of your womb, Jesus, O clement, O loving, O sweet Virgin Mary. Amen."

5. **The Memorare.** "Remember, O most gracious Virgin Mary, that never was it known that anyone who fled to your protection, implored your help, or sought your intercession was left unaided. Inspired by this confidence, I fly unto you, O Virgin of virgins, my Mother. To you I come, before you I stand, sinful and

sorrowful. O Mother of the Word Incarnate, despise not my petitions, but, in your mercy, hear and answer me. Amen."

6. **Seven Hail Marys in honor of the Seven Sorrows of Mary.** Mary has promised very special graces to those who do this on a daily basis. Included in the promises of Our Lady for those who practice this devotion is her pledge to give special assistance at the hour of death, including the sight of her face. The seven sorrows are:

(1) The first sorrow: the prophecy of Simeon (Hail Mary).
(2) The second sorrow: the flight into Egypt (Hail Mary).
(3) The third sorrow: the loss of the Child Jesus in the temple (Hail Mary).
(4) The fourth sorrow: Jesus and Mary meet on the way to the cross (Hail Mary).
(5) The fifth sorrow: Jesus dies on the cross (Hail Mary).
(6) The sixth sorrow: Jesus is taken down from the cross and laid in Mary's arms (Hail Mary).
(7) The seventh sorrow: the burial of Jesus (Hail Mary).

7. **Litany of the Blessed Virgin Mary.**
Lord, have mercy on us.
   Christ, have mercy on us.
Lord, have mercy on us. Christ, hear us.
   Christ, graciously hear us.
God, the Father of heaven, *have mercy on us.*
God, the Son, Redeemer of the world,
   have mercy on us.
God, the Holy Spirit, *have mercy on us.*
Holy Trinity, one God, *have mercy on us.*
Holy Mary, *pray for us* (repeat after each invocation).

Holy Mother of God,
Holy Virgin of virgins,
Mother of Christ,
Mother of the Church,
Mother of divine grace,
Mother most pure,
Mother most chaste,
Mother inviolate,
Mother undefiled,
Mother most amiable,
Mother most admirable,
Mother of good counsel,
Mother of our Creator,
Mother of our Savior,
Virgin most prudent,
Virgin most venerable,
Virgin most renowned,
Virgin most powerful,
Virgin most merciful,
Virgin most faithful,
Mirror of justice,
Seat of wisdom,
Cause of our joy,
Spiritual vessel,
Vessel of honor,
Singular vessel of devotion,
Mystical rose,
Tower of David,
Tower of ivory,
House of gold,
Ark of the Covenant,
Gate of heaven,
Morning star,
Health of the sick,
Refuge of sinners,

Comforter of the afflicted,
Help of Christians,
Queen of angels,
Queen of patriarchs,
Queen of prophets,
Queen of apostles,
Queen of martyrs,
Queen of confessors,
Queen of virgins,
Queen of all saints,
Queen conceived without original sin,
Queen assumed into heaven,
Queen of the most holy rosary,
Queen of families,
Queen of peace,
Lamb of God, who take away the sins of the world,
spare us, O Lord.
Lamb of God, who take away the sins of the world,
graciously hear us, O Lord.
Lamb of God, who take away the sins of the world,
have mercy on us.
Pray for us, O holy Mother of God,
that we may be made worthy of the promises of Christ.

Let us pray: Grant, we beseech You, O Lord God, that we Your servants may enjoy perpetual health of mind and body and, by the glorious intercession of the blessed Mary, ever virgin, be delivered from present sorrow, and obtain eternal joy. Through Christ our Lord. Amen.

We fly to your patronage, O holy Mother of God. Despise not our petitions in our necessities, but deliver us always from all dangers, O glorious and blessed Virgin. Amen.

8. **Prayer to St. Joseph.** St. Joseph, guardian of Jesus and

chaste spouse of Mary, you passed your life in perfect fulfillment of duty. You supported the Holy Family of Nazareth with the work of your hands. Kindly protect those who trustingly turn to you. You know their aspirations, their hardships, their hopes; and they turn to you because they know you will understand and protect them. You too have known trial, labor, and weariness. But, even amid the worries of material life, your soul was filled with deep peace and sang out in true joy through intimacy with the Son of God entrusted to you, and with Mary, His tender Mother. Amen.

— *(Pope John XXIII)*

9. **Litany of the Sacred Heart, promises of the Sacred Heart.**
   Lord, have mercy on us.
   Christ, have mercy on us.
   Lord, have mercy on us. Christ, hear us.
   Christ, graciously hear us.
   God the Father of heaven,
   have mercy on us (repeat after each invocation).
   God the Son, Redeemer of the world,
   God the Holy Spirit,
   Holy Trinity, one God,
   Heart of Jesus, Son of the eternal Father,
   Heart of Jesus, formed by the Holy Spirit in the womb of the Virgin Mother,
   Heart of Jesus, substantially united to the Word of God,
   Heart of Jesus, of infinite majesty,
   Heart of Jesus, sacred temple of God,
   Heart of Jesus, tabernacle of the Most High,
   Heart of Jesus, house of God and gate of heaven,
   Heart of Jesus, burning furnace of charity,
   Heart of Jesus, abode of justice and love,
   Heart of Jesus, full of goodness and love,
   Heart of Jesus, abyss of all virtues,

Heart of Jesus, most worthy of all praise,
Heart of Jesus, king and center of all hearts,
Heart of Jesus, in whom are all the treasures of wisdom
and knowledge,
Heart of Jesus, in whom dwells the fullness of divinity,
Heart of Jesus, in whom the Father is well pleased,
Heart of Jesus, of whose fullness we have all
received,
Heart of Jesus, desire of the everlasting hills,
Heart of Jesus, patient and most merciful,
Heart of Jesus, enriching all who invoke You,
Heart of Jesus, fountain of life and holiness,
Heart of Jesus, propitiation for our sins,
Heart of Jesus, loaded down with opprobrium,
Heart of Jesus, bruised for our offenses,
Heart of Jesus, obedient even to death,
Heart of Jesus, pierced with a lance,
Heart of Jesus, source of all consolation,
Heart of Jesus, our life and reconciliation,
Heart of Jesus, victim of sin,
Heart of Jesus, salvation of those who hope in You,
Heart of Jesus, hope of those who die in You,
Heart of Jesus, delight of all the saints,
Lamb of God, Who take away the sins of the world,
spare us, O Lord.
Lamb of God, Who take away the sins of the world,
graciously hear us, O Lord.
Lamb of God, Who take away the sins of the world,
have mercy on us.
Jesus, meek and humble of heart,
make our hearts like unto Yours.

Let us pray: O almighty and eternal God, look upon
the Heart of Your dearly beloved Son and upon the praise
and satisfaction He offers You in behalf of sinners and,
being appeased, grant pardon to those who seek Your

mercy, in the name of the same Jesus Christ, Your Son, Who lives and reigns with You, in the unity of the Holy Spirit, world without end. Amen.

Promises of Our Lord to those devoted to His Sacred Heart (these should be read by the prayer leader):

(1) I will give them all the graces necessary in their state of life.

(2) I will establish peace in their homes.

(3) I will comfort them in all their afflictions.

(4) I will be their refuge during life and above all in death.

(5) I will bestow a large blessing on all their undertakings.

(6) Sinners shall find in My Heart the source and the infinite ocean of mercy.

(7) Tepid souls shall grow fervent.

(8) Fervent souls shall quickly mount to high perfection.

(9) I will bless every place where a picture of My Heart shall be set up and honored.

(10) I will give to priests the gift of touching the most hardened hearts.

(11) Those who promote this devotion shall have their names written in My Heart, never to be blotted out.

(12) I promise you in the excessive mercy of My Heart that My all-powerful love will grant to all those who communicate on the first Friday in nine consecutive months the grace of final penitence; they shall not die in My disgrace nor without receiving their sacraments; My divine Heart shall be their safe refuge in this last moment.

10. **Prayer for Priests.** "Lord Jesus, Chief Shepherd of the Flock, we pray that in the great love and mercy of Your Sacred Heart You attend to all the needs of Your priest-shepherds throughout the world. We ask that You draw

back to Your Heart all those priests who have seriously strayed from Your path, that You rekindle the desire for holiness in the hearts of those priests who have become lukewarm, and that You continue to give Your fervent priests the desire for the highest holiness. United with Your Heart and Mary's Heart, we ask that You take this petition to Your heavenly Father in the unity of the Holy Spirit. Amen."

11. **Prayer for all members of the Shepherds of Christ Associates.** "Dear Jesus, we ask Your special blessings on all members of Shepherds of Christ Associates. Continue to enlighten them regarding the very special privilege and responsibility you have given them as members of Your movement, Shepherds of Christ Associates. Draw them ever closer to Your Heart and to Your Mother's Heart. Allow them to more and more realize the great and special love of Your Hearts for each of them as unique individuals. Give them the grace to respond to Your love and Mary's love with an increased love of their own. As they dwell in Your Heart and Mary's Heart, abundantly care for all their needs and those of their loved ones. We make our prayer through You to the Father, in the Holy Spirit, with Mary our Mother at our side. Amen."

12. **Prayer for the spiritual and financial success of the priestly newsletter.** "Father, we ask Your special blessings upon the priestly newsletter, Shepherds of Christ. We ask that You open the priest-readers to the graces You wish to give them through this chosen instrument of Your Son. We also ask that You provide for the financial needs of the newsletter and the Shepherds of Christ Associates. We make our prayer through Jesus, in the Holy Spirit, with Mary at our side. Amen."

13. **Prayer for all members of the human family.**
"Heavenly Father, we ask Your blessings on all Your children the world over. Attend to all their needs. We ask Your special assistance for all those marginalized people, all those who are so neglected and forgotten. United with our Mother Mary, we make this petition to You through Jesus and in the Holy Spirit. Amen."

14. **Prayer to St. Michael and our Guardian Angels:**
"St. Michael the Archangel, defend us in battle. Be our safeguard against the wickedness and snares of the devil. May God rebuke him, we humbly pray, and do thou, O prince of the heavenly hosts, by the power of God, cast into hell Satan and all the other evil spirits who prowl about the world seeking the ruin of souls. Amen."
"Angel of God, my guardian dear, to whom God's love commits me here, ever this day be at my side, to light and guard, to rule and guide. Amen."

15. **Pause for silent, personal prayer.** This should last at least five minutes.

16. **Act of consecration to the Sacred Heart of Jesus and the Immaculate Heart of Mary.**

"Lord Jesus, Chief Shepherd of the flock, I consecrate myself to Your most Sacred Heart. From Your pierced Heart the Church was born, the Church You have called me, as a member of Shepherds of Christ Associates, to serve in a most special way. You reveal Your Heart as a symbol of Your love in all its aspects, including Your most special love for me, whom You have chosen as Your companion in this most important work. Help me to always love You in return. Help me to give myself entirely to You. Help me always to pour out my life in love of God and neighbor! Heart of Jesus, I place my trust in You!

"Dear Blessed Virgin Mary, I consecrate myself to your maternal and Immaculate Heart, this Heart which is symbol of your life of love. You are the Mother of my Savior. You are also my Mother. You love me with a most special love as a member of Shepherds of Christ Associates, a movement created by your Son as a powerful instrument for the renewal of the Church and the world. In a return of love, I give myself entirely to your motherly love and protection. You followed Jesus perfectly. You are His first and perfect disciple. Teach me to imitate you in the putting on of Christ. Be my motherly intercessor so that, through your Immaculate Heart, I may be guided to an ever closer union with the pierced Heart of Jesus, Chief Shepherd of the flock."

17. **Daily Prayers.** All members should say the Holy Spirit prayer daily and make the act of consecration daily. They should also pray the rosary each day. They are encouraged to use the other above prayers as time allows.

Other great books
published
by
Shepherds of Christ
Publications

To order any of the following materials please contact us by mail, phone, fax, email or the Internet:

Shepherds of Christ Publications
P.O. Box 627
China, Indiana 47250 USA

Toll free USA: (888) 211-3041
Tel: (812) 273-8405   Fax: (812) 273-3182
Email: info@sofc.org   http://www.sofc.org

Please contact us for *Prayer Manuals* or to begin a Prayer Chapter to pray for the priests, the Church and the world.

C1. *The Word Alive in Our Hearts*
Homilies by the Reverand Joe
Robinson given at St. Boniface
Church in Cincinnati, Ohio. It is
a tremendous honor Fr. Joe has
allowed us to share these great
gifts with you – for greater
holiness and knowing more and
more about God. $5

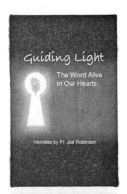

C2. *Focusing on the Word - Cycle B*
Homilies by the Reverand Joe
Robinson given at St. Boniface
Church in Cincinnati, Ohio. This
is the complete Liturgical Cycle B.
It is a tremendous honor Fr. Joe
has allowed us to share these
great gifts with you – for greater
holiness and knowing more and
more about God. $10

B8. *Mass Book*, by Rita Ring: Many of
the entries in the Priestly
Newsletter Volume II from a
spiritual journal came from this
book. These entries are to help
people to be more deeply united to
God in the Mass. This book is
available in English and Spanish
with the Church's *Imprimatur.* $12

BN4. *Response to God's Love* by Fr.
Edward J. Carter, S.J. In this book
Fr. Carter speaks of God as the
ultimate mystery. We can meditate
on the interior life of the Trinity.
Fr. Carter tells us about our unique-
ness in the Father's Plan for us,
how the individual Christian, the
Church and the world are in the
state of becoming. *Imprimatur.* $10

BN3. *Shepherds of Christ - Volume 3* by Fr. Edward J. Carter, S.J. Contains Newsletter Issues 1 through 4 of 2000 including Fr. Carter's tremendous *Overview of the Spiritual Life* $10

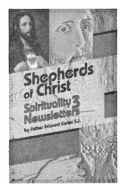

BN2. *Shepherds of Christ - Volume 2*: by Fr. Edward J. Carter, S.J. Contains issues 13-29 of the newsletter (September/October 1996 - Issue 5, 1999) $15

BN1. *Shepherds of Christ - Selected Writings on Spirituality for all People* as Published in Shepherds of Christ Newsletter for Priests. Contains 12 issues of the newsletter from July/August 1994 to May/June 1996. $15

B7. *Rosary Meditations for Parents and Children,* by Rita Ring, Short Meditations for both parents and children to be used when praying the rosary. These meditations will help all to know the lives of Jesus and Mary alive in their Hearts. Available in both English and Spanish with the Church's *Imprimatur.* $10

Shepherds of Christ Ministries

<u>Send Order To:</u>
Shepherds of Christ Ministries
P.O. Box 627
China, Indiana 47250 USA

<u>Order Form</u>

	<u>Qty</u>	<u>Total $</u>
P1. Prayer Manuals	____	____
C1. The Word Alive in Our Hearts ($5)	____	____
C2. Focusing on the Word - Cycle B ($10)	____	____
C3. Feed My Soul - Cycle C ($10)	____	____
B8. Mass Book ($12)	____	____
BN4. Response to God's Love ($10)	____	____
BN3. Shepherds of Christ - Volume 3 ($10)	____	____
BN2. Shepherds of Christ - Volume 2 ($15)	____	____
BN1. Shepherds of Christ - Volume 1 ($15)	____	____
B7. Rosary Meditations for Parents and Children ($10)	____	____
Totals:	____	____

Name: _____

Address: _____

City: _____ State: _____ Zip: _____

For More Information Call Toll free USA: 1-888-211-3041

Shepherds of Christ Ministries

<u>Send Order To:</u>
Shepherds of Christ Ministries
P.O. Box 627
China, Indiana 47250 USA

<u>Order Form</u>

	<u>Qty</u>	<u>Total $</u>
P1. Prayer Manuals	___	_____
C1. The Word Alive in Our Hearts ($5)	___	_____
C2. Focusing on the Word - Cycle B ($10)	___	_____
C3. Feed My Soul - Cycle C ($10)	___	_____
B8. Mass Book ($12)	___	_____
BN4. Response to God's Love ($10)	___	_____
BN3. Shepherds of Christ - Volume 3 ($10)	___	_____
BN2. Shepherds of Christ - Volume 2 ($15)	___	_____
BN1. Shepherds of Christ - Volume 1 ($15)	___	_____
B7. Rosary Meditations for Parents and Children ($10)	___	_____
Totals:	___	_____

Name: _____

Address: _____

City: _____ State: _____ Zip: _____

For More Information Call Toll free USA: 1-888-211-3041